A Pictorial History of
SUTHERLAND SHIRE

Joan Lawrence

Captions Pauline Curby

KINGSCLEAR BOOKS

To Mary, Denis Jennifer + Susan Hope you enjoyed your trip Dave + Catriona

COVER PHOTOGRAPH:

The Cecil Hotel, 1937. This, Cronulla's premier hotel in the 1930s and 1940s, was opened in 1927 when the owner C O J (Joe) Monro upgraded and extended an older building, Monro Flats. In the post-war years, as Cronulla changed from a holiday resort to a residential suburb, the hotel lost much of its elegance and was known best as a beachside drinking spot. It was demolished in 1988 to make way for the Cecil Apartments. The facade of the old hotel has been retained. (GPO, Mitchell Library)

BACK COVER PHOTOGRAPH:

The Cronulla periscope, photographed by M C Hinder, c. 1915. Arthur Rickard, described as the "biggest speculative subdivider" in Sydney at this time, advertised his development of Beach Park Estate (located between Hume, Mitchell, Elouera and Wyanbah Roads) on the side of this building. Rickard visualised real estate opportunities where others saw only uninhabited sandhills. (GPO, Mitchell Library)

© Kingsclear Books ACN 001 904 034
3/77 Willoughby Rd, Crows Nest 2065
Ph: (02) 9439 5093 Fax: (02) 9439 0430

© Copyright 1997 Kingsclear Books
Reprinted 1998 (twice)

ISBN 0 908272 52 9

Design and Artwork by New Frontier Creative Services (02) 9876 1050

Printed by Pirie Printers Pty Limited, Canberra.

The area now called the Sutherland Shire (incorporated 1906) was officially founded by Government Proclamation in 1835 and named. Previously, the area had been unofficially known as The Southern Land or The Southern District; and was one of several Southern Districts – all unofficially recognised – stretching as far as the Port Phillip District (now Victoria).

Journal of the Royal Australian Historical Society
No. 69, May, 1968

Preface

The Sutherland Shire covers 370 square kilometres and is often referred to as the birthplace of modern Australia for within its area lies Kurnell where Lieutenant (later Captain) James Cook arrived and landed from the *Endeavour* in 1770. The shores of Botany Bay very nearly became the site for the first white settlement on the continent but insufficient shelter for the ships of the First Fleet in 1788, and the lack of a good supply of fresh water, forced Governor Arthur Phillip to seek an alternative site. He selected Sydney Cove within Sydney Harbour beside the banks of the stream named the Tank Stream. Nevertheless the Sutherland Shire has many historical associations from those early days. Settlement in the area developed leading to the proclamation of local government on 6 March 1906 by the then Governor of New South Wales, Admiral Sir Harry Holdsworth Rawson.

The shire has vast areas of native bushland which includes the Royal National Park, Australia's first national park. Residents and visitors may also enjoy any of the four surfing beaches of Cronulla, North Cronulla, Elouera and Wanda and sports people may pursue almost every sport or recreational activity popular in Australia.

A population boom occurred in the 1950s, soon after the end of World War II, and the shire continues to grow with increasing housing areas and the creation of new suburbs. This book offers an overview of the development of the Sutherland Shire in text and photographs.

Acknowledgements

Various organisations and people are to be acknowledged and thanked for assistance in the preparation of this book: the research facilities of the Mitchell Library, State Library of New South Wales; the library of the Royal Australian Historical Society; use has also been made of the collection of Quarterly Bulletins of the Sutherland Shire Historical Society held by the Mitchell Library and the RAHS; the collection of newspaper cuttings and articles of the publishers Kingsclear Books; Aileen Griffiths, of Cronulla; Ian Robinson of Robinson's Pharmacy, Gymea; Steven Crampton of Gymea; Alf Kerr of Carlingford; Jon Breen of Australian Water Technologies; Cronulla Surf Club; Denise Bray, Librarian, Garrawarra Centre for Aged Care, Waterfall; Don Bowden, Gymea Bowling Club; pamphlets from National Parks and Wildlife Service; Bettye Ross, President, St George Historical Society Inc; Ron Lawrence of Cromer; Pauline Curby for reading the manuscript and contributing the captions; and Catherine Warne, Kingsclear Books, for helping to collect and copy photographs and produce the book.

Photographs were obtained from *Sydney Illustrated News*, Small Pictures File, and the Government Printing Office records, Mitchell Library and the Dixon Library; the Government Printer in Harris Street, 1984; Lee Thompson, Sutherland Hospital Caringbah; Steven Crampton of Gymea; Pam Goesch of Castle Cove; Sydney Water Archives, Croydon Park; Ivan Webber, Board of Woronora Cemetery; John Veage, *St George and Sutherland Shire Leader*; the descendants of John Hill; Cronulla Surf Club; the Railway Historical Society; permission to use the still from *Forty Thousand Horsemen*, directed by Charles Chauvel, was granted by Curtis Brown (Aust) Pty Ltd, Sydney; the National Film and Sound Archives; and the Kingsclear Books collection.

For those who wish to delve further into the history of Sutherland Shire the local Historical Society (founded in 1966) and Local History Section at Sutherland Library are recommended. Both have diligently collected and preserved the shire's historical heritage in written and photographic form.

Contents

The Dharawal Language People

Living in what is now the Sutherland Shire were various Aboriginal groups. The Eora (meaning "the people") language group lived around Sydney and the coastal area north of Botany Bay. On the southern shore of Botany Bay with territory covering much of the Cronulla-Sutherland peninsula were the Dharawal, a smaller linguistic group than the Eora. Within the Dharawal or Tharawal group were a number of smaller clans comprising the Bidjigal (or Bediagal) centred around Salt Pan Creek, Bankstown, on the Georges River, Revesby, Georges Hall, Chester Hill, Chullora, Beverly Hills and Oatley. The Norongerragal were located at Sandy Point and Mill Creek but they ranged south of the Georges River and west of the Woronora River. The Gweagal were around North Cronulla close to fresh water lakes and to Woolooware, Quibray and Weeney Bays and Cronulla Beach. The Gweagal were the furthest north horde of the Dharawal speaking people from the south. Their territory also extended north of Port Hacking and west to Sutherland and, some claim, to Shoalhaven and west to Berrima and Camden.

Archaeological evidence discloses the people of the Georges River area fished with hooks and lines and barbed fishing spears. Their food supply included oysters, fish, eels, platypus, kangaroos,

This photograph labelled "the last five full bloods" was taken on Thomas Holt's estate c. 1888. Although few Dharawal people survived the invasion of their country, there was a small Aboriginal community in what is now Sutherland Shire in the 19th century. One visitor to the district described how "the old dark girl Biddy Giles" (pictured here) had acted as a guide to him and his companions in the 1860s. (Rockdale Library)

wallabies, reptiles, possums, birds, honey, birds' eggs, wild figs, yams, fern roots, cabbage tree palm hearts and bulbs of certain lilies. They left behind various middens in rocky overhangs such as those at Little Moon and Great Moon Bays, Alfords Point and Illawong, at Sylvania, Oatley Point, Connell's Point, Lime Kiln Bay and Lugarno. One of the largest was in Jewfish Bay, now within Oatley Park.

In the early 1780s, far away in England, a group of men discussed the formation of a British colony at Botany Bay in New Holland. Sir Joseph Banks and Lord Sandwich are believed to be among the first to discuss the idea but another closely related with the development of a definite plan was James Matra (remembered in the Sydney suburb of Matraville).

Matra (d. 1806) was born in New York, the

son of American loyalists who moved to Canada following the American War of Independence. James was a member of Cook's *Endeavour* in 1770, initially as able seaman, then midshipman and was entered in the ship's books as Jas Magoa. On 23 August 1783 he addressed the British government on "A Proposal for establishing a settlement in New South Wales … to atone for the loss of our American colonies".

Both Sir Joseph Banks and Matra, in discussions on New South Wales as a possible site for a colony, stated that the indigenous people were few in number. Matra declared New South Wales was "peopled only by a few black inhabitants, who, in the rudest state of society, knew no other arts than such as were necessary to their mere animal existence, and which was almost entirely sustained by catching fish". Banks in April, 1779 said there would be little opposition from these people. In 1770 (during Cook's voyage):

He saw very few, and did not think there were above Fifty in all the Neighbourhood, and had Reason to believe the Country was very thinly peopled; those he saw were naked, treacherous, and armed with Lances, but extremely cowardly, and constantly retired from our People when they made the least Appearance of Resistance.

(Testimony to the House of Commons Committee on the Return of Felons)

The truth was that the population of the Port Jackson – Botany Bay area (now estimated in the region of Sydney and suburbs to have been between 5,000 to 8,000) was already supporting the maximum population for a hunter – gatherer economy.

Aboriginal occupancy of the Sydney – Illawarra area has been dated to between 5,000 to 7,000 years ago and its society, both economic and with religious links to the land, had been functioning generations before the white intrusion.

Various archaeological studies and research has been carried out in Sutherland Shire. At Captain Cook's landing place at Kurnell a large midden revealed a concentration of mud oysters. In fact, Cook commented "on vast heaps of the largest oysters" he had ever seen. Also discovered were fragments of bottle glass, an iron nail and bone button consistent with gifts made during the white visits of 1770 and 1788. Rock shelters, too, have revealed artefacts such as a bone point and gouge; a fish-hook file, engraving and pebble tools, shells and bones.

Surgeon Arthur Bowes Smyth (1760-1790) of the *Lady Penrhyn* with the First Fleet had a special interest in nature and the Aborigines and in his journal (1787-1789) gives a description of the local people, probably the Gweagal. On 21 January 1788 during a visit to the south side of Botany Bay. He wrote:

They were all perfectly naked rather slender, made of a dark black colour, their hair not woolly, but short & curly, – Every one had the tooth next the fore tooth in his upper jaw knock'd out, & many of them had a piece of stick abt. The size of a Tobacco pipe & 6 or 8 inches in length run thro' the septum of the Nostrils, to wh. from its great similitude we ludicrously gave the name of a Sprit Sail Yard.

They cut their Backs Bodies & Arm wh. heal up in large ridges & scars.

In 1868 Archbishop W.B. Ullathorne (1806-1889) in his autobiography recorded an account of a talk with two members of a Botany Bay tribe concerning the arrival of Captain Cook at Botany Bay:

When they saw the two ships they thought them to be great birds. They took the men upon them in their clothes, and the officers and marines in their cocked hats, for strange animals. When the wings (that is, the sails were closed up), and the men went aloft, and they saw their tails hanging down [sailors wore pigtails in those days] they took them for long-tailed opossums. When the boat came to land, the women were much frightened; they cried and tried to keep the men back. The men had plenty of spears, and would go on. Cook took a branch from a tree and held it up. They came on, and they trembled. Then Cook took out a bottle and drank and gave them it to drink. They spat it out – salt water! It was their first taste of rum. Cook took some biscuit and ate it, and gave them some. They spat it out – something dry! It was the old ship-biscuit. Then Cook took a tomahawk and chopped a tree. They liked the tomahawk and took it. Thus the first gift they saw the value of was the axe that was destined to clear their woods and to make way for the white man. Allowing for the broken English, that is an accurate narrative of the tradition of the Botany Bay tribe.

Long before Ullathorne's recollections, the Spanish explorer Don Alexandra Malaspina with two vessels, the *Descuvierta* and *Atrevida*, arrived in Sydney Harbour having been sent to investigate the new English colony. He accused the British government of usurping the rights of the natives and other European nations. He felt the colony had been founded in defiance of his own nation's prior rights in international law. He also saw the effects colonisation was having and would have on the indigenous people of the Pacific and in Sydney. He exposed the contradiction in the claim of bringing the benefits of civilisation to the indigenous people and reflected on the consequences observing "what will be easier and sooner will be the destruction rather than the civilization of these unhappy people".

The Botanists of Botany Bay

At 2 pm on Sunday 29 April 1770 the 330 ton barque *Endeavour*, a former Whitby collier, sailed and anchored in Botany Bay. At 3 pm the same day a party in two boats led by James Cook approached a rock on the southern headland of the bay. Cook was in fact a Lieutenant being promoted to the rank of Captain on 17 April 1775 following his second voyage of discovery.

Two Aborigines rushed down to the landing party, shouted, gesticulated wildly, brandished their spears and shouted "Warra, Warra, Wai" (meaning "go away, go away"). Cook made gestures to the Aborigines and offered beads, nails and other gifts "... which they [the Aborigines] took up and seemed not ill pleased with". But as the boats advanced the Aborigines again opposed the intrusion. Cook ordered a musket to be fired between the men and one retaliated and hurled a stone into the boat. Cook again ordered musket shots fired, one blast of small shot struck one man in the leg. The Aborigines ran to their "huts".

A well-known portrait of Sir Joseph Banks in later life. (Government Printer)

Cook effected the landing and tradition states that Isaac Smith, a young cousin of Cook's wife, Elizabeth, was the first to leap ashore. The two Aborigines, protected with shields, returned and hurled their spears at the sailors. Musket fire resounded and a spear whistled through the air as the Aborigines vanished "to the woods".

The landing party entered the Aborigines' shelters and souvenired about 50 spears leaving in their place beads, cloth and ribbons. Failing to locate fresh water the landing party returned to the *Endeavour*. The next day Cook's party returned and located the fresh water stream and discovered the gifts left in the "hut" were still there unwanted.

The *Endeavour* spent eight days at Botany Bay. Captain Cook and his botanists carefully examined the country. Initially named Sting-Rays Harbour, Cook changed the bay's name to Botanist Bay, then to Botany Bay because of "the great quantity of New Plants &ca. Mr Banks & Dr Solander collected in this place".

Joseph Banks (1743-1820) was 27 years of age when he arrived at Botany Bay. He had been educated at Harrow, Eton and attended Christ Church, Oxford. He claimed he was first interested in botany at Eton, through the beauty of the local wildflowers. During leisure time he was an avid reader of Greek and Latin so as to glean greater knowledge about plant life. By the age of 21 he was a gentleman of considerable means and would go botanising and fishing with a friend, Lord Sandwich.

It was the Royal Society that urged the Admiralty to allow Banks to accompany Captain Cook on his voyage to the South Seas. Banks had a staff of eight: Dr Daniel Carl Solander and H D Spiring, naturalists; Alexander Buchan and Sydney Parkinson, landscape and natural history artists; James Roberts and Peter Briscoe, tenants from the Banks' family home; Revesby Abbey, Lincolnshire, Thomas Richmond and George Dorlton (or Dollin) negro servants. Banks, Solander and the two Revesby men were the only survivors, from this party, after the voyage. Banks' two servants were frozen to death during the *Endeavour's* passage around Cape Horn.

Banks' party was well equipped for collecting, studying and preserving their specimens. They also carried "a fine library of Natural History" as well as machines for catching and preserving insects, nets, trawls, drags and hooks for coral fishing, plus a type of telescope for observing through water to a great depth. There were cases of bottles with spirits to preserve animals, salts to store seeds, and wax. Solander claimed Banks contributed £10,000 to the expedition.

Solander (1736-1782), son of a Swedish clergyman, had been a pupil of the famous botanist Carolus Linnaeus. Solander was an Assistant Librarian at the British Museum and in 1764 was elected a Fellow of the Royal Society. He met Banks who engaged him for the voyage on the *Endeavour* at £400 a year. When the ship returned to England Solander became Banks' secretary and librarian, later receiving an honorary degree as doctor of civil law from the University of Oxford. Described as "... a rather short, plump man of some thirteen stone, jovial, fond of company and much in demand in London society," Solander was deeply distressed at the marriage of Linnaeus's eldest daughter,

Dr Daniel Carl Solander, a Swedish naturalist on the Endeavour's *voyage of 1770. (Government Printer)*

Elisabeth Christina, and became a confirmed bachelor. He died of a stroke on 13 May 1782. Dr Edward Duyker researching *Daniel Solander, Collected Correspondence 1753-1782* claims Solander was involved in industrial espionage. "He made a number of study tours, looking at aspects of glass-making and metal-founding. He tried to recruit ... Matthew Boulton, who together with James Watt later developed the steam engine, for Swedish industry. So Solander was under surveillance by the British authorities".

At sea the naturalists had studied their books but also collected fish, crustaceans, molluscs, coelenterates and birds. All were examined, described, sketched and preserved but the strange vegetation of Botany Bay fascinated Joseph Banks and his botanists. They collected a vast variety of plants new to science.

After the *Endeavour* sailed from Botany Bay the beaching of the ship at Endeavour River (Queensland) caused water to flow to the stern of the vessel, destroying some of the plant specimens. Collections and observations had been made at Rio de Janeiro, Tierra del Fuego, Tahiti and New Zealand, Botany Bay and Endeavour River. Banks wrote, "the collection of plants was ... grown so immensely large that it was necessary that some extraordinary care should be taken of them least they should spoil in the books".

At the entrance to Botany Bay the headlands are named Cape Banks and Point Solander. Solander is also remembered with a monument at Kurnell, a tropical American plant genus *Solandra*; some Australian plant species, an island in New Zealand plus a book-box, "the Solander case" for carrying notes and specimens.

Sir Joseph Banks by middle-age held a unique position in the scientific and social world of England and was requested to voice an opinion on a variety of subjects. He maintained a life-long interest and influence in the colony of New South Wales and became known as the "father of Australia". He is remembered in numerous monuments, street names, the Sydney suburbs of Banksia, Banksmeadow and Bankstown and the Banksia, a genus of the family *Proteaceae* which contains over 50 species of shrubs and small trees, the first specimens of which were collected by Banks on the shores of Botany Bay.

The Arrival at Botany Bay in 1788

In consequence of the decision of the British Prime Minister William Pitt's Cabinet in 1786 to found a penal settlement at Botany Bay, the British Admiralty was instructed on 31 August the same year, by Lord Sydney, Secretary of the Home Department (which dealt with colonial affairs), to commission the fleet. Evan Nepean, Secretary of the Admiralty, had estimated the cost for founding the settlement at £29,300 and that it would cost £18,669 to run it the first year, £15,449 the second and £7,000 the third and then it should be self victualling.

The *Supply*, with Governor-elect Captain Arthur Phillip, arrived at Botany Bay at 2.15 pm on 18 January 1788, two days ahead of the remainder of the ships. At 3 pm the "boats were hoisted out" for the first landing by Phillip, Lieutenants King and Dawes and other officers of the *Supply* who went ashore to explore the north side of bay. At daylight the next day King and others again went to the northern shore to haul the net, caught very few fish, but met some Aborigines. They noted their fires on Cape Banks and saw a great many "Indians" on Cape Solander, who shouted and shook their weapons at the visitors. Later in the morning Phillip, King, Major Ross, Lieutenants Ball, Dawes and

Long, in three boats, explored for about six miles the river at the north-west side of the bay. The party found the country low and boggy and no appearance of fresh water. They returned and then explored along the upper part of the bay to the entrance of the first inlet on the south-west side of the bay, which they noted was very wide in this part. Here they went ashore and "… eat our salt beef and, in a glass of porter, drank the healths of our friends in England".

By the 20 January 1788 all 11 ships of the fleet were at Botany Bay and anchored off the site of Kurnell. A marine officer, Captain Watkin Tench, noted in his journal, "that by 10 o'clock … the whole of the fleet had cast anchor … after a passage of exactly thirty-six weeks from Portsmouth". The distance sailed was 15,063 miles.

Exploration of the area continued and Phillip, the Lieutenant Governor and Captain Hunter went to the south side of the bay on the 20 January, "little within Point Sutherland". King, Dawes and three marines explored all the south side of the bay and traced the two inlets "on the south side as high as possible". King named the highest hill Lance Point which he climbed and found "the soil an exceeding fine black mold, with some excellent Timber Trees & very rich grass". He also noted "a red fox dog" and saw a "number of the natives, who halloo'd & made signs for us to return to our boats". In the evening Surgeon Arthur Bowes Smyth of the *Lady Penrhyn* went to the north side of the bay and caught "a great many fish" and considered that at first sight it looked "a most fertile spot" but on closer inspection found the grass:

long and coarse, the trees very large and in general hollow, and the wood itself fit for no purposes of building or anything but the fire. The soil to a great depth is nothing but black sand.

Phillip, too, was disappointed with Botany Bay. The water supply was insufficient for a settlement, the bay afforded little shelter to the ships and the "green meadows" noted by Captain Cook in 1770 were not to be found. Neither stores nor convicts were landed. Phillip, with Captain Hunter and a small party, set out in ship's boats to explore Port Jackson to the north. Meanwhile Major Ross and his marines started to clear Point Sutherland in case the area had to be used for the settlement. Phillip wanted saw pits dug but it was noted "it appeared worse the lower down we went, and in digging a sawpit, the whole depth of it was little else but sand, and swamps all around". Ross also explored with Dr Arndell and Lieutenant Clark and the latter noted in his journal, "After walking a great way, sat down to dinner with what we had brought with us when Arendell [sic] by accident ran the kniff through his hand. I bound it up and stopped the blood". Somewhat disillusioned with Botany Bay Clark commented "I hope that the Commd will find out a better place at Port Jackson for us to settle, for if we are oblige to settle here, as the place they intend, there will not a soul be a life in the course of a year".

Phillip returned on 23 January much impressed with Port Jackson and decided to move the Fleet to Sydney Cove. The shore party which had completed the saw pit was instructed to bring the timber frame to the ship and the masters ordered to prepare their vessels for sea immediately. On the 24, as the fleet prepared to leave, there was consternation when two ships were noted approaching the bay. The sighting at first was greeted with disbelief, then rumour. "They were Dutchmen sent to dispossess us, and the moment after storeships from England, with supplies for the settlement" (Tench). The ships' arrival caused the delay of the departure of the First Fleet from Botany Bay as Phillip wanted to be certain of their identity. They were unable to enter the bay because of the weather conditions and it was not until the 26 January their entrance was achieved. It was Phillip who ascertained they were French ships on a voyage of discovery in the southern hemisphere. The *Boussole* and *Astrolabe* were under the command of Jean-Francois de Galaup, Count of Laperouse, and the expedition spent six weeks at Botany Bay before sailing away. The wrecks of the ships were discovered on the reefs of Vanikoro, in the Solomon Islands, many years later. The arrival of the ships caused Phillip to hurriedly have the English colours hoisted on the 24 January on the southern side of Botany Bay, near the watering place at Sutherland Point.

After Governor Phillip decided to move the Fleet to Port Jackson, Tench noted his observations of Botany Bay prior to their departure:

The Bay is very open, and greatly exposed to the fury of the S.E. winds, which, when they blow, cause a heavy and dangerous swell. It is of prodigious extent, the principal arm, which takes a S.W. direction, being not less,

William Bradley's depiction of the First Fleet entering Botany Bay on the 21 January 1788. (SPF, Mitchell Library)

including its windings, than twenty-four miles from the capes which form the entrance, according to the report of the French officers, who took uncommon pains to survey it.

The fleet was clear of Botany Bay by 3 pm on 26 January, but all experienced difficulty in working out of the bay, "everyone blaming the rashness of the Governor in insisting upon the fleet working out in such weather" (Bowes Smyth). They arrived at Port Jackson about 7 pm.

Although the First Fleet established the settlement at Sydney Cove, Botany Bay was not neglected for small parties of officers tramped to Botany Bay to dine with the French officers. La Perouse also returned escaped convicts who made their way back to Botany Bay in the hope of escaping with the French.

In September 1788 Phillip sent Captain John Hunter and a party of men, including Watkin Tench, back to Botany Bay to survey both the bay and the mouth of the Georges River. The same year Lieutenant William Bradley mapped the Woronora River. It was Hunter in 1795, when he was Governor of New South Wales, who gave permission for the voyage of Matthew Flinders and George Bass in the little boat of 8-foot keel, *Tom Thumb*, to explore both Botany Bay and the Georges River. They took with them Bass's servant, William Martin and the voyage lasted nine days. They made a favourable report to Hunter on what they had observed. They made another voyage to the area in 1796, again with Martin, but in a slighter, larger *Tom Thumb*.

For 18 months after the settlement was founded a weekly party of marines was sent to Botany Bay in case a ship arrived, ignorant of the removal to Port Jackson. The practice was discontinued when a signal was established on South Head at Sydney. With the establishment at Sydney Cove, Botany Bay diminished in importance.

Henry Hacking and Port Hacking

Gundamaian, circa 1890, was a restful, secluded spot in the National Park with good fishing close at hand. Nearby was "Wentworth's Hut" where the Deer Park ranger lived. This was later removed and replaced by the more substantial dwelling, Gundamaian. (Mitchell Library)

Henry Hacking (c. 1750-1831) was a first fleeter, quartermaster of *HMS Sirius*, flagship of the fleet. Hacking had considerable skill as a "good shot" and gained knowledge of the bush while hunting.

Judge Advocate David Collins (1756-1810) noted Hacking was held "in great estimation by the officers of his ship, both as a man and as a seaman". Hacking is believed to have returned to England in 1790 following the wreck of the *Sirius* but returned to Sydney on the *Royal Admiral* in 1792. By 1794 he was one who attempted to cross the barrier of the Blue Mountains claiming to have travelled 20 miles further inland than other explorers. The following year he was one of the party to discover the lost cattle at the Cowpastures (now Camden) and he also explored the region south-west of Parramatta. He had a varied career, was granted land at Hunters Hill and also sent by Governor Hunter to examine salt deposits near the Bargo and Nepean Rivers. However in October 1799 he was convicted of perjury and sentenced to transportation on Norfolk Island, but was later granted an absolute pardon.

In 1802 Hacking was first mate on the *Lady Nelson* which accompanied Matthew Flinders on the *Investigator* when it sailed to North Queensland. Hacking left the *Lady Nelson* in 1803 and became a pilot on Sydney Harbour but his career plummeted when he was accused of stealing material from the *Investigator*, then in the harbour. Despite his pleas that the goods were going to waste, Hacking was found guilty and sentenced to death. Hacking was granted a reprieve on condition he was transported to Van Diemen's Land (Tasmania) for seven years. By that time David Collins was Lieutenant Governor of that colony and he availed himself of Hacking's "well known abilities as a Pilot". Governor King wrote to Collins in 1804 "I am glad you have kept Hacking, he is a good man but lost here by the Arts of a Woman" (in 1803 Hacking had shot and wounded a woman, for which he received a reprieve).

Hacking became coxswain to the Lieutenant Governor and in 1806 appointed pilot at Hobart. He continued his exploratory skills visiting the Huon Valley in 1804. In Van Diemen's Land he rose to the post of Harbour Master and Pilot. When he retired in 1816 Hacking was found "useless as a Pilot from Drunkenness and other infirmities" but granted a pension of half his salary. He died at Hobart in his eighty-first year on 21 July 1831.

It appears that Hacking was not the first white discoverer of the port which bears his name. It is claimed to have been sighted by a seaman from *HMS Supply*, James Aicken, when seeking water for the First Fleet. The area became known as Port Aiken and Port Aiken Heads until c. 1870. Earlier, in 1796, when Bass and Flinders, with the boy Martin, explored the area in the second *Tom Thumb* they sighted and named Port Hacking for Henry Hacking. Flinders stated Hacking had originally told them of its existence. On this voyage Bass and Flinders travelled as far south as Lake Illawarra and nearly lost their lives in a gale. The Aborigines called the Port Hacking area Deeban, remembered in the Deeban Spit, off Maianbar.

Port Hacking, sighted and named in the early days of white settlement, eventually became a recreational facility for both residents and visitors. The small suburb of the same name is located between Burraneer Bay and Little Turriell Bay on the shores of Port Hacking and nestled between the suburbs of Dolans Bay and Lilli Pilli. In 1840, 20 acres of land on the point was held by Francis Mitchell and the parish map names the point "Great Turriell" or "Lilly Pilly Point". Politician and landowner, Thomas Holt also held an adjoining grant marked on the map as "Lilli Pilli in the Village of Port Hacking". Dolans Bay bears the name of a pioneer, Patrick Dolan, who purchased land in the area in 1856. His son, Dominick, also purchased land and built a stone cottage c. 1865. Lilli Pilli was originally part of Dominick Dolan's farm and was subdivided from 1909. Large scale residential development occurred in the 1950s and 1960s, when original homes such as Moombara and Nuimburra were cut up into smaller lots. The first public school opened in Lilli Pilli in 1957. Robert Cooper Walker, in a report in 1868, mentioned the area in a description of Thomas Holt's estate stating "there is another small point, called 'Lilly Pilly Point' on account of the native myrtles that grow there, in rich black soil". The berries of the beautiful lilly pilly (*Acmena smithii*) were a food source for the Aborigines.

Winifred Falls, circa 1890.
This relaxing spot in the
Royal National Park is located
a little past the head of
navigation of South West Arm.
(SPF, Mitchell Library)

Kurnell – Captain Cook's Landing Place

Now a suburb within Sutherland Shire, Kurnell is famous as the 1770 landing place of Captain (then Lieutenant) James Cook.

The Kurnell Peninsula is on the eastern-most extremity of the shire and 324 hectares of the area, known as Captain Cook's Landing Place, lies within Botany Bay National Park. In 1899 to commemorate Cook's landing, 248 acres were dedicated as a public recreation area and named. Politician Joseph Hector McNeil Carruthers, Premier of New South Wales in 1904, was appointed chairman of the trustees to administer the area. The area was later extended and since 1967 has been maintained by the National Parks & Wildlife Service. There is an excellent Discovery Centre and numerous historic sites to visit. In the vicinity of the creek known as "Cook's Watering Place" is the burial place of the British seaman from the *Endeavour*, Forby Sutherland.

Sutherland hailed from the Orkney islands off the northern-most tip of Scotland, an area which provided numerous seamen to the British merchant and Royal Navy. In May 1770 Sutherland succumbed to tuberculosis and was buried at Kurnell far from his native land. Richard Pickersgill, master's mate on the *Endeavour* said Sutherland was afflicted with consumption "ever since our departure from Streights le Maire" and Sydney Parkinson recorded he was "decently interred". Elias Laycock, son of pioneer John Connell Laycock, remembered when he was a child an old Aboriginal woman, Sally Mettymong aged about 85 to 90 years, who would walk him along the little beach immediately below the Solander monument and point up the slope stating "white man buried there". She had vivid recollections when she was a girl of seeing Captain Cook's ship come in and a party land at Kurnell. Cook named Point Sutherland in honour of the seaman. The shire also has a Forby Sutherland Memorial Garden which is a memorial to the men of the *Endeavour*.

Cook described the area as "well-wooded" but the ancient trees have been removed although the Sydney red gum *Angophora costata*, scribbly gum *Eucalyptus haemastoma* and the wooden pear *Xyomelum pyriforma*, survive. The cliff tops support a rich coastal heathland with numerous wildflowers in spring, which attract nectar and seed eating birds.

On 10 June 1815 Governor Macquarie promised 700 acres, portion 1, to Captain James Birnie. The grant was verified by Surveyor Dixon in 1827. Birnie named the property Alpha (or

Thomas Holt, landowner and politician, erected this monument in 1870 to celebrate the centenary of James Cook's landing on the southern shores of Botany Bay. This site (now part of Botany Bay National Park) was at this time part of Holt's extensive estate. In 1899 the land was resumed for the creation of a public park. (Mitchell Library)

First) Farm with an annual quit rent of 14 shillings conditional on his cultivation of 60 acres of his holding. He never resided on the property but appointed a manager and was issued convict labour.

There was a three-room cottage on the property. A ship's captain, Birnie made several trading visits to Sydney before he settled in the town and became a senior partner in James Birnie & Co, a ships' chandlers with whaling and sealing interests. Birnie's physical and mental health deteriorated and his wife, Martha Matilda, sought a Deed of Separation stating, because of her husband's violence, she had been "obliged to seek a temporary home".

The 1828 census lists Birnie as 66 years, arrived on the *Mary Ann* in 1809 and resided as a merchant in O'Connell Street. The same year Birnie was "pronounced lunatik" and his estate placed under the control of two members of the Legislative Council. Alpha Farm was sold in 1828 by the trustees to another merchant, John Connell, senior. The Deed of Separation Birnie's wife applied for did not take place and Martha Matilda remained with her husband until his death on 14 July 1844 at the age of 82 years. He was buried by the Reverend J D Lang in the Devonshire Street Cemetery. Mrs Birnie survived, infirm and nearly blind, until November 1851 and was buried with her husband. When Central Railway was established on the cemetery site in 1901 their bones and headstone were removed to Botany Cemetery.

On 31 March 1821 portions 2 and 3 at Kurnell were promised by Governor Macquarie to John Connell. John Connell, senior, his son, John and daughter, Margaret, arrived on the *Marquis Cornwallis* in 1802. Connell's wife, Catherine, had been transported for 14 years and the family had chosen to accompany her to the colony. On arrival Catherine was assigned as a servant to her husband and later given a conditional pardon. Connell, senior, became a merchant in Sydney but his wife died on 7 May 1811.

The *Sydney Gazette* carries reference to this effect on 11 May and on 25 May reports that Mrs Catherine Connell died on Tuesday night "after a long and painful illness; to which she submitted with exemplary patience and true Christian resignation". It further states she was the wife of Mr John Connell "of Pitt Street, aged 50 years; & leaves an affectionate Husband and young family to lament her loss".

There is some confusion as to whether portions 2 and 3 were granted to Connell senior or junior. As the father was a well-established merchant in Sydney it was assumed the land was given to his son. M. Hutton Neve in *The Early Days of Kurnell to Cronulla* (1983) states that research suggests that the assumption that Connell, junior, received the land is incorrect. A John Connell was given:

on promise in 1821 1,000 acres commencing at Woolooware Bay, on the south by a line west one hundred and fifty chains, on the west by a line north seventy chains and on the north by a line east one hundred and fifty chains and Gawley [sic] Bay, Being the Land promised to Gregory Blaxland.

Also a grant:

on promise of 180 acres in the Parish of Sutherland Bounded on the west by a line North, forty two chains, on the North by George's River; On the East by that River, and on the South by Gawley [sic] Bay and a Creek running into that Bay.

John Connell, senior, acquired Alpha Farm in 1828. On his death in 1849 his estate was left to his two grandsons, John Connell Laycock and Elias Pearson Laycock, sons of his daughter Margaret and her husband, Captain Thomas Laycock, junior, of Bringelly. The grandsons shared the property, John chose the Kurnell area and Elias the Woolooware property.

Gangs of grass cutters cut the grass in the area which was shipped to Sydney for stock when other areas were suffering from drought and, apparently, John Connell, junior, cut the timber on the property clearing most of Kurnell and Woolooware. The Connell land covered some 1,790 acres. Alpha Farm was known for its fruit and vegetables, and cattle-raising, and later operated as a dairy.

Elias Laycock, son of J C Laycock, in the RAHS Journal No.10 of 1924 recalled his father "coping in 80 head of dairy cattle on the foreshores of Kurnell, hauling them by means of ropes to the ship's sides, and having them hoisted to the deck of the vessel to be shipped to the Clarence". When Elias was 12 years old the family moved to the Clarence River and owned a station, Glenreagh. His father had been a member of the Legislative Assembly in Sydney and after the move north, he represented that district in parliament. Elias also remembered that below the Solander monument at Kurnell was a ship's dock, or channel, cut by Captain Birnie to bring his boats right up to the shore. J C Laycock also held large tracts of land in the Caringbah – Burraneer Bay area bought during crown land sales from 1856 to 1858.

Fernleigh, their stone house at Burraneer Bay, was probably built by John Connell Laycock some time between 1850 and 1860 although the date is uncertain despite it bearing the date MDCCCXXI (1821). It is felt this inscription date, perhaps, only commemorates the first land grant to the Connell family. J C Laycock's son, Elias, stated their property was mortgaged to purchase the Prince of Wales Theatre (later the Theatre Royal) which was destroyed by fire. The insurance was "faulty" and Laycock lost his money. As well as the theatre Laycock lost in the fire, his George Street iron foundries, a bakery and other businesses were under-insured. Elias further stated his father sold his Botany land, including Alpha Farm, to Thomas Holt for £3,000 (five shillings per acre). Holt had inspected the property with J C Laycock and his son, Elias, and at the auction in 1861 bid £3,275 for 4,600 acres. Elias Laycock became a famous sculler, trained on Port Hacking and became an Australian champion in 1875 and 1879.

The first surveys were carried out by Surveyor John Dixon in 1827 who was instructed by Surveyor General John Oxley to commence "the survey of the outer South Head of Botany Bay, and carefully trace the Shore thereof to Georges River". Dixon was further instructed to "trace the Coast to Port Hacking with all its branches [and to] particularly note the extent of the Sand Shoals off Port Hacking and the line of direction of the Fairway of the Channel". Dixon's surveys were scrapped on the appointment of Thomas Mitchell as Surveyor General following Oxley's death.

It is usually accepted that Kurnell was named from the corruption of Connell but it has also been suggested that it may also be a corruption of an Aboriginal word. Thomas Holt acquired a vast estate stretching to Sutherland but he was a great enthusiast of Kurnell claiming it to be "Australia's Plymouth Rock". It was Holt who erected the monument to Captain Cook at Kurnell in April 1870 to commemorate the centenary of Cook's landing and the historic significance of the area.

Kurnell – From Settlers to Port Botany

Early settlers attracted to the southern region of Sydney were the shell gatherers and timber getters. Aboriginal middens and natural shells were collected to obtain the lime necessary for mortar for buildings in the settlement. Kurnell also attracted fishermen as Botany Bay supported various species of fish and by the late 19th century Kurnell was a small fishing village. Even up to the time of the depression, fishermen's shacks dotted the area, a peaceful escape, but during the depression a shanty town developed as a refuge for those left homeless and unemployed. A sandy track ran along the edge of swamps at the base of the sandhills near Quibray Bay giving rough access to Cronulla.

For nearly 25 years the SS Erina, an 82 foot long with 18 foot maximum beam vessel, operated a regular weekend passenger service from Sans Souci to Kurnell, with stops at Brighton-le-Sands and Botany. The service commenced on 7 November 1903 and was operated by Messrs Skidmore and Childs. Captain Thomas Childs was in charge of the Erina for most of the years it operated on Botany Bay. Originally built at Gosford, on the central coast, the Erina was considered the best sea-going vessel built in that district. The service proved popular with church groups and was used in regattas with fares of one shilling return or nine pence for the single trip. The service sadly closed on Easter Monday, 1927, as it was no longer viable.

There had been several subdivisions of land in Kurnell prior to World War I. In May 1926 the Silver Beach Estate at Kurnell was opened for private sale and there was a phenomenal response with over 100 inquiries within a few days and more than 60 blocks sold in a single weekend. It was disclosed one of the earliest buyers was "a gentleman on a visit to Sydney from Switzerland" who purchased nine blocks. It was estimated the entire subdivision would be

The monument to La Perouse on the northern side of Botany Bay from the Sydney Illustrated News, *16 June 1866. (Mitchell Library)*

sold in a few weeks. Blocks ranged in price from £50 upwards and overlooked Botany Bay, impinging "on a delightful stretch of silvery beach".

During the 1940s Sam Latta operated a bus service along the bumpy, rough cart road, sometimes through king tides and bush fires. Once, along the ridge of the Kurnell Peninsula, were huge sand dunes. Filmmaker Charles Chauvel, in the early 1940s, used the dunes in the production of his epic *Forty Thousand Horsemen* concerning the Australian Light Horse campaign in Palestine during World War I.

It was also during the 1940s that mining of the sandhills began for use by the construction and metropolitan industries. Approximately 2.5 million tonnes were extracted annually until the sandhills dwindled away. The peaks of the dunes were also used by hang-glider enthusiasts for practice purposes. In January 1997 Sutherland Shire voted to halt development on the Kurnell Peninsula including the mining of 1.5 million tonnes of sand. However, in April 1997 heritage authorities called for protection of the last of Kurnell's sand dunes which escaped the sandmining when 30 million tonnes of sand was stripped from the peninsula. The dune close to the Towra Point tidal wetlands and home to Sydney's last significant populations of the endangered green and golden bell frog was under threat from a $50 million resort project.

The matter was in the provence of the Land and Environment Court. Sutherland Shire Council had requested an urgent commission of inquiry to review a number of large developments for the area including sandmining, the resort with a nine-hole golf course and a 330 room hotel, an upgrade of the Cronulla sewage treatment plant and an electrical co-generation plant at the Ampol refinery. The New South Wales government refused the council's request for the inquiry. The council had received over 2,000 public objections to the resort to be constructed by Australand Pty Ltd and delayed its decision to consider the objections. Australand Pty Ltd appealed to the Land and Environment Court and Sutherland Shire Council later rejected the resort plans. The National Trust of Australia (NSW) considered Kurnell of "vital heritage importance to the nation" and the dune an "integral and essential element of the peninulsa".

Post World War II industry made inroads into the Kurnell Peninsula with the establishment of Australian Oil Refinery, a lubricating refinery and chemical laboratories, and in the 1960s modern homes were being constructed at Kurnell.

In the 1960s, with a change in shipping to container vessels, the Maritime Services Board saw inadequacies in Port Jackson including the lack of large areas of land close to the wharves to unload, store and transport the containers. In 1961 the Board was granted control of the navigable waters of Botany Bay and in 1962 recommended, following a research programme, that the new port be built on the northern foreshores of Botany Bay. The work was approved by the State government, and the Maritime Services Board reclaimed an area of tidal mud flats for a large hydraulic model of the bay to simulate wave conditions. In 1971 construction of the new port began amid protests about the dredging and the effects on marine and bird life, the prawning and oyster industries.

The Botany Bay Port and Environmental Enquiry was instituted under the new State Labor government in 1976. Although the enquiry recommended the port proceed, it was recommended the work be confined to the first phase, with the exclusion of the Coal Loader and the VLCC (Very Large Crude Carrier) Berth. The port transport proposals should be replanned with rail transport considered, the ecological and environmental resources of the area to be recognised and protected, and overall planning to be controlled and co-ordinated by the Planning and Environment Commission. Large-scale developments in Botany Bay inevitably affect the natural systems with changes to land, shores and water systems.

In the 1960s there was a plan to build a new airport on Towra Point but this scheme was abandoned. The announcement was made by Prime Minister John D. Gorton at a press conference at Kingsford-Smith Airport on 29 March 1968 and the decision was seen as a triumph for public opinion. The Towra Point Nature Reserve was gazetted in 1974. By the mid 1980s there were further protests about environmental concerns on the Kurnell Peninsula and the importance of the Towra Point wetlands.

The Kurnell Action Committee called for the area to be kept free of toxic pollutants pointing out 176 birds species had been recorded in the Towra Point area and that the viability of the wetland flora and fauna depended on the maintenance of good water quality. In 1988 the Towra Point wetlands became part of a national park area.

Botany Bay as it appeared in the Sydney Illustrated News *on 23 September 1854. (Mitchell Library)*

Thomas Holt of Sutherland (1811-1888)

Thomas Holt was born at Horbury, Yorkshire, England on 14 November 1811, the eldest son of 13 children born to a Leeds wool merchant Thomas Holt and his wife, Elizabeth (nee Ellis). Young Thomas received his education at the Pontrefact Academy and from the Reverend Cope at Wakefield. At 14 years he was destined to enter his father's business to become a wool buyer and travelled the wool markets of Europe. By 1835 he was a partner in his father's firm and with a brother, William, established a branch firm in Berlin, Germany. On 20 March 1841 he married the daughter of a German merchant, Sophie Johanna Charlotte Marie Eulert.

Attracted to the Colony of New South Wales after reading Dr J D Lang's *Historical and Statistical Account,* Holt, his wife, a lady's maid and two employees arrived in Sydney on board the *Helvellyn* on 16 November 1842. He was soon a succcessful wool buyer but also became a magistrate and a real estate speculator and was recognised as one of the colony's prominent financiers.

He was both a friend and business associate of Thomas Sutcliffe Mort (1816-1878), both men being involved in the founding of the AMP

Society and Sydney Insurance Company, the Hunter River Railway, the Sydney Railway Company and the Australian Joint Stock Bank. Holt was involved in many business concerns and built a family home at Liverpool, Sophienburg. Here the Holts were visited by Caroline Chisholm and were friends of explorer, Ludwig Leichhardt, who became the godfather of their son, Frederick Samuel Ellis. In 1855 Holt retired from active business but retained his directorships.

Holt further acquired pastoralist interests in both New South Wales and Queensland, holding some 3,000,000 acres by 1880. His business and interests were wide and varied. In 1856 he won Stanley Boroughs in the first Legislative Assembly, later becoming Colonial Treasurer. He was interested in education and was said to be "addicted to writing to newspapers". He sought improvements to immigration, swamp drainage and the refrigeration of food.

Holt acquired 82 acres in Rocky Point Road in the Parish of St George and lobbied politicians to obtain water from the Georges River to help provide an adequate water supply for Sydney, one of his favourite causes. He built several homes including Camden Villa at Newtown, Sans Souci on his land between Kogarah Bay and Botany Bay and The Warren at Marrickville on an estate of 130 acres. Here Holt introduced 60 wild rabbits from England which bred prolifically and caused

a nuisance although a paper of the day declared "… we are glad to hear that an attempt is now being made to raise a scale to introduce the wild rabbit on the estate of Mr Holt at Cook's River. These are enterprises that enrich a country and enhance its attractions."

Thomas Holt (1811-1888), landowner and politician, acquired a large part of what is now Sutherland Shire in the early 1860s. This land monopoly was one of the factors that delayed settlement of the district for a number of years. (GPO, Mitchell Library)

Following the gold rush era Holt disposed of some of his pastoral runs and in August 1861 acquired land at Kurnell and eventually held an area from Botany Bay to Georges River, to Port Hacking and west to the Woronora River, some 12,000 acres, known as the Holt-Sutherland Estate. At Kurnell there was a cottage named Kurnell or Curnell's. However, his first headquarters were at Miranda where he had a lucerne farm and the first men to join him as overseers were William Simpson and John Lehane.

Holt endeavoured to raise sheep on his pastures but dingoes played havoc with his flocks. Holt had poison laid around Bottle Forest (Heathcote) and 300 dingoes were destroyed. However, the land was unsuitable for sheep and many suffered from footrot. On Holt's orders 13,000 sheep were destroyed and buried on Towra Point with layers of seaweed placed between the rotting animals to aid the process and act as a fertiliser.

Holt brought cattle from his Queensland station in his own craft the *Delaware* and unloaded them at his wharf in Gwawley Bay. Again the country was not suitable for cattle and stock were lost through snake bites.

Holt imported the first buffalo grass from America which he planted himself while inspecting the estate and also placed small bags of the seed on the necks of his sheep to be dropped while they grazed. Timber getting was the most successful venture as there was fine ironbark and blackbutt which he shipped from Sylvania to Sydney and yielded £5,000. Holt spent vast sums pioneering scientific oyster farming and also investigated coal mining as it was said a portion of the Bulli coal seam ran through the district.

In the 1870s Holt served on the Council of Education and visited, as a Commissioner for Exhibitions, Philadelphia (1876), Paris (1878) and Amsterdam (1883). He was indefatigable in his activities and interests being a vice president of the Agricultural Society of New South Wales and a member of the Royal Society of New South Wales.

During the 1870s Thomas Holt promoted the need for an Illawarra railway which would benefit the colony but would also benefit Holt as a large landholder. In 1879 Holt's wife and daughters left Sydney to spend some time abroad. During the 1870s Holt began construction of another mansion, Sutherland House, on the shores of Sylvania. It was completed in 1881. Holt sold the Warren at Marrickville in 1880 and moved the contents, including rare books and artworks to Sutherland House. The driveway to the house ran along the shores of Gwawley Bay. Sutherland House and 700 acres was given to his son, Frederick "and his heirs in perpetuity".

Holt resided with son and family until he left for Europe in 1881. The entailment of the property to Frederick's heirs was broken by Act of parliament following Frederick's death in 1902.

After Frederick Holt and his family left the property in 1897 the house became Sylvania Sanatorium. On Easter Monday, 20 April 1908, Sutherland House was offered for auction with a leaflet describing the property as having 39 rooms with:

no fewer than 16 bedrooms off one corridor alone, most of the 16 opening onto the balcony which overlooks the bay ... Every one of them is large, roomy, well-ventilated ... The dining room measures 36 feet by 27 feet, and opens out onto the (glass walled) conservatory, which in its turn gives access to the beautiful well kept garden, and commands views of George's River and Botany Bay almost from La Perouse to Tom Ugly's Point. There are maid's rooms, men's rooms, two kitchens, gentlemen's and ladies' bathrooms and lavatories; carpenter, smith and painter's shops, and the most wonderfully arranged motor garage, stabling, cow bails and fowl houses. A never ending supply of the purest spring water is raised by the medium of the windmill.

Several families lived on the property and Holt kept them supplied with milk, butter, eggs and vegetables and at Christmas there was always a gift for everyone, on the Holt family Christmas tree. The property also included a wharf and boatsheds and Holt built swimming pools and dressing sheds.

Sutherland House became a guest house with successive owners. In 1911 it was proposed as an Australian Naval College but rejected because of shallow water in the bay.

Eventually a caretaker was placed in charge but the house was destroyed by fire on 17 December 1918. Three years previously Sutherland House had been purchased for £3,000, insured for £2,000 and furniture for £1,000.

The Propeller newspaper in December 1918 reported the caretaker, Richard Matehurn Griffiths, left the property at 5 pm to go to a nearby store and on his return noticed the fire. He thought it had been deliberately lit in his absence and a witness stated he looked at the fire at 6.30 pm with field glasses and saw two men on the parapet at the front of the house. The Coroner returned an open verdict.

The house was later demolished and Sutherland council bought 4,000 feet of dressed stone and 8,000 bricks for £39. The stone was used for road building, in a retaining wall along the Georges River and in three war memorials. The carriageway of the property is now Belgrave Esplanade and the old swimming baths and dressing pavilion are part of Lachlan and Bogan Avenues, and Murray Island.

In 1881 Holt returned to England where he devoted the remainder of his life to the poor of London, aiding the work of the Salvation Army (he was, himself, a Congregationalist) and Dr Barnardo. Even in the year of his death, 1888, he published *Christianity, or the Poor Man's Friend.* Thomas Holt died at his home, Halcot, Bexley, County Kent on 5 September survived by his wife, Sophie and three sons and three daughters. He left an estate valued at nearly £330,000.

Holt is also remembered in the Thomas Holt Memorial Village at North Sutherland. Ten acres of land was donated by Thomas A. Holt, in Acacia Road, for a retirement settlement.

Early Industry

The abundance of shells and Aboriginal middens attracted early shell gatherers to Botany Bay and the southern area. In Sydney building with bricks and sandstone required lime as both the mortar and stucco were lime-based mixtures. In Britain limestone burnt at intense temperatures was used but in the colony the lime was obtained by burning shells. The practice continued through to the 1860s.

Shell gathering was a poor person's occupation and a hard life. As middens were depleted shells were gathered from rocks or from tidal mudflats and the gatherer was often knee deep in water. Convicts carrying bags of lime suffered when the substance ran into the scars of flogged men. There was a public kiln on Bennelong Point, now the site of the Sydney Opera House, and Cockle Bay shellfish were burnt at kilns on Darling Harbour with lime merchants located along the waterfront. Shells gathered from Brisbane Water and Pittwater to the north of Sydney and Botany Bay to the south were shipped to and burnt at Millers Point. There was once a Lime Street, south of Erskine Street and west of Sussex Street. which commemorated the lime-burners. On occasions the shell gatherers had their boats confiscated by the authorities when shells, timber "or anything else they could lay their hands on" was taken illegally off private estates. Under the Seaman's Act boats were required to have the owner's name painted in an "eligible situation" but the requirement was not always complied with.

One of the shell gatherers was a well known Queensland identity, Captain William Collin. He and an old shipmate named Massey camped at Port Hacking in 1856 and began collecting shells which they sold to schooners and ketches. Here they made the acquaintance of Gogerly who Collin described as a "curious old gentleman, formerly editor of a Sydney newspaper, cast into prison for two years for libel". Collin and Massey also claimed, on one occasion, Gogerly told them he saw a "yahoo" or wild man in the woods, "12 feet high and carrying a staff 20 feet long". Collin believed it was a ruse to frighten them away but they took their guns and went in search. They claimed to have found some remarkable tracks but no sign of the "yahoo".

Fishermen were also attracted to the southern area because of the quantity of fish. The first reference was made in the *Sydney Gazette* of 14 December 1806, "On Friday a boatload of salted fish, amounting to 13 cwt. was brought in at the Hospital Wharf, the whole procured at and about Port Aikin in the space of eight days, and very

Botany Bay in 1851, like the Sutherland Shire area, attracted fishermen and shell gatherers. (SPF, Mitchell Library)

well preserved". Hospital Wharf was in the area of today's West Circular Quay and Port Aikin is the earlier name for Port Hacking. Fishing was often the first attraction for settlement as happened at the village of Gunnamatta, later Cronulla, in the 1860s. By the 1880s most of the Georges River, Woronora River and Port Hacking were closed to netting fish, either permanently or periodically, although in a report of the Commissioners of Fisheries of 1888 it was reported that fish of all kinds were "abundantly supplied" and mullet were in "enormous shoals". The Woronora River had whiting, flathead and red bream, and prawns were caught in winter. There was an abundance of prawns in the Georges River, Botany Bay and Cooks River.

The area became famous for its oysters and divers collected mud and rock oysters diving to depths of 15 feet without equipment. It was an important industry in the shire with, at one time, 104 oyster leases employing 50 men. The total area of foreshore farms covered 61,587 yards and the area of offshore farms covered 557 acres. In 1949 production reached 8,511 bags, or 358,656 pounds, and the yearly value of production was £60,000. On the Georges River and Port Hacking area some 60 men were engaged in the industry with 129 boats. Even in the 1980s some 20,000 bags, each containing 100 dozen oysters, were produced annually. The industry netted millions of dollars until struck by the QX (Queensland unknown) virus, and pollution resulting in the closure of many leases.

From the earliest days the virgin forests attracted the timber getters and sawmillers. The clay soils of the Sutherland area were originally covered with a turpentine and ironbark forest, but included blackbutt, grey ironbark, red mahogany and white stringybark. Between 1815 and 1840 the Connell family were clearing their property from Kurnell to Woolooware. In the 1830s John Connell cut a channel from the northern end of Woolaware Road to the bay to take his timber by boat to Sydney. Thomas Holt sold large quantities of his timber between 1862 and 1868 but as Cridland in *The Story of Port Hacking, Cronulla and Sutherland Shire* noted "the scrub was cleared and the useless timber ringbarked to permit more grass to grow, the earth only sent up a prolific crop of seedlings that reduced the original scanty herbage". Holt also cleared the mangroves and saltmarsh in Gwawley Bay and drained the head of the bay to establish canals for his venture in oyster farming. Near Cronulla, in the 1860s, there was still ironbark, grey and white gum, mahogany and stringybark. Robert Cooper Walker in the Sutherland Estate Report, 1868, reported that the Port Hacking area was still "heavily timbered with gum, Stringy Bark, Bloodwood and Mahogany … but a good deal has been cut down for fencing and other purposes". He further noted "some of the other land is poor barren scrubby land in high undulating country covered with honeysuckle". This was in the area of today's Sylvania Heights and the honeysuckle is the banksia.

When Thomas Holt acquired his land he took out mining rights as it was believed the Bulli coal seam passed under Sutherland. James Murphy had been a mining speculator and had imported a diamond-drilling machine from the United States of America exhibited at Sydney's Great Exhibition in 1879. Thomas Holt and Murphy formed a syndicate to discover a payable coal seam on the Holt property. The syndicate carried the cost of the bores to find a profitable seam of coal and in return had a 56 years' lease at a yearly rental. Explorations were carried out between 1879-1880 and the first spot chosen to bore was about 300 yards north of the later site of the Cronulla Hotel, and the second at Harnett's paddock near the banks of a creek (that crossed Kingsway at the intersection with Dolans Road). Despite reaching a depth of 1,500 feet no coal was found. The third attempt was nearer to Sutherland on Dents Creek at the head of the north-west arm of Port Hacking. After reaching 2,000 feet, coal was discovered, a seam 4 feet 8 inches of good grade Bulli quality. It was gauged the seam was about 11 feet but proof was inconclusive. The bore operations ceased on Holt's estate but Murphy formed a reconstructed syndicate and leased Holt's lands and formed the Holt-Sutherland Estate Land Company Ltd. For over 40 years Murphy was secretary, manager or director of Holt-Sutherland Estate and planned the roads when the estate was subdivided. He later founded Como and built Como House, which was destroyed by fire in 1969, and operated the Como Pleasure Grounds. Murphy died in 1924 and in his will gave the proceeds of his Sutherland property to assist needy university students in agricultural research, "particularly with regard to the hybridization of Australian plants" (Cridland).

In 1888 a timber merchant of Pyrmont, Sydney William Burns, senior, moved to

Rockdale and opened an agency and Burns Timber Yard in Sutherland. By 1910 he had acquired 3 acres in Caringbah and opened another timber yard. Following his death the business was continued by his son, William Joseph Burns, who had a property on the corner of President Avenue and Kingsway opposite his timber yard. Timber was brought from Sutherland by steam tram which ran beside the timber yard and timber was offloaded over the fence. The timber yard existed until 1953 but as Caringbah grew it was unsuitable for a timber mill. Burns sold the site to the city store, McDowell's, and their new store opened in November, 1961. Burns' sons continued the business at The Boulevarde.

The Sutherland brick works opened c. 1890 and made sandstock bricks in an open kiln. Clay was obtained from near today's Woronora Crematorium and the bricks used in numerous local buildings. The brick works closed after a few years because of competition and Bakewell Bros opened claypits at Heathcote. Heathcote was then Bottle Forest, an area of about 200 acres.

Heathcote Hall was constructed from Bakewell bricks in 1883 by a brick master Isaac Harber and was a Victorian-style house with a central tower which gave superb views over the district. Between 1912 and 1917 the Sutherland Brick Company Ltd operated at Sutherland, with a siding at the works for the Sutherland – Cronulla steam tram to serve the brick works. After the company went into voluntary liquidation it was taken over by Refractory Bricks Ltd. In 1927 it was sold to Punchbowl Brick and Tile Co Ltd with a branch at Heathcote. Miranda Fair expanded

in 1992 to the largest shopping complex in the southern hemisphere, but once in the vicinity was a market garden and a brick making claypit. The old pit was filled in and Woolworths Ltd was built on the site when Miranda Fair initially opened in 1964.

When Sutherland Shire was declared under the Local Government Act in 1906, the shire consisted of many fruit, vegetable and poultry farmers, clay brick diggers and railway workers and their families. The population at that time was about 1,500 but by the outbreak of World War II it had reached 19,500. The shire's development and population explosion occurred following World War II at such a rate that even the redoubtable Thomas Holt would have been astounded.

The Pioneers

*F*ollowing in the footsteps of the shell gatherers, timber getters, fishermen, Captain Birnie and the Connells, came others hopeful of securing a living in these remote areas. Initially access to the southern districts was by vessels down the coast. Many of the early settlers selected land at Port Hacking which was accessible by water.

Prior to 1830 the Governor was able to grant land to encourage emancipated convicts and free settlers to farm. Title to the land was only given after it was surveyed. Among the early landholders

Samuel Elyard's view of Botany Bay, no date, showing the isolated development in Botany Bay c. 1860, an area which, like Sutherland Shire, was not good for farming. (SPF, Mitchell Library)

given land by either grant or purchase were Owen Byrne in 1821, his son Andrew in 1825 and Matthew John Gibbons in 1824. All land was south of Port Hacking. Also, in 1823, John Lucas was granted 150 acres on the Woronora River. Nathaniel Lucas and his family had a mill at Liverpool which was sold on his death in 1818. His son, John, established a water-driven mill adjacent to the ford on the Woronora River and it was operating by 1826, grinding grain for local farmers. Small vessels were able to negotiate the river to collect milled grain and return by the Georges River to Botany Bay. The mill was destroyed by fire in the 1830s.

Another of the pioneers was Charles James Gogerly, a convict transported for life, who arrived in Sydney in 1819. A 1991 quarterly bulletin of Sutherland Shire Historical Society discloses more facts on Gogerly. He had been an attorney's clerk in London but was assigned as labourer to John Warby in the Airds District. He had a ticket-of-leave in 1831 and a conditional pardon in 1838. In 1841 he was at Mullet Creek, Illawarra District, with his wife, a son and two daughters. By 1842 he was back in Sydney at Brinkley's Alley, off Kent Street. In 1843 Gogerly suddenly became a publisher of a newspaper, *The Omnibus & Sydney Spectator*, which originally appeared in 1841 but then lapsed. Apparently it was a scurrilous paper publishing true or false scandalous tales. Gogerly soon faced court for obscene libel but was, it appears, only a front for an unrevealed publisher. Nevertheless, Gogerly was given a sentence of 12 months and sent to Newcastle. By 1851 he was back in Sydney as a general dealer at 331 Pitt Street. About the same time he acquired land at Port Hacking and was a resident there in 1854.

Captain William Collin, who encountered Gogerly around 1856, said his family was the only one living at Port Hacking and that he maintained a garden of potatoes, maize and fruit trees and lived opposite Lilli Pilli. Collin also commented the that area was infested with dingoes and wild cattle. Gogerly is remembered in the point which bears his name at Lilli Pilli and by his cottage, one of the earliest buildings in the Sutherland area, a single storey residence where he lived with his wife, Charlotte and their children (see the study of Gogerly's cottage by Terry Kass).

On Christmas Eve 1864 Gogerly was implicated in a boating tragedy while rowing home in company with the Molloy family. The

P H F Phelps, sketcher and settler, did this drawing of a bark hut on the Georges River drawn between 1840 and 1865. It depicts the type of housing pioneers lived in. There was little development in what is now Sutherland Shire until the opening of the Illawarra line in 1885. (SPF, Mitchell Library)

two flat-bottomed dinghies in which Gogerly, the Molloys and Thomas Potter were travelling carried Christmas supplies. However, the men had been drinking and Potter rowed close to Gogerly's vessel to pass a bottle of rum. Grasping the bottle Gogerly managed to upturn his vessel plunging the passengers into the water. Endeavouring to save himself, the other boat also capsized and the only survivors of the incident were Gogerly and young John Molloy. By 1879 Gogerly was living in Newtown with his daughters where the family operated a drapery business. He used some of his land at Port Hacking to raise loans for the business and eventually the land was sold to a Sydney solicitor.

In 1858 Mary and Andrew Webster bought 108¾ acres of land at the head of Burraneer Bay for £108.15s with a yearly quit rent of a peppercorn. In 1862 James Wilson paid £252 for 252 acres but his survey showed only 169 acres and he was given another 83 acres. He later sold his land to Thomas Holt. Dominick Dolan purchased the Webster land in 1863 and built a small stone cottage. Dominick, a son of Patrick Dolan who had land in the area of Dolans Bay, remained a bachelor, and after his death in 1888, his land was subdivided and sold at auction. Lilli Pilli was part of Dolan's farm and residential development began sparsely from 1909.

Two of the first residents to build houses at Port Hacking were Jack Want and Critchett Walker. Walker had the only telephone and bore the cost of the erection of the poles from Tom Uglys to Turriell Bay. An early resident, Mrs Simpson, was an elderly woman who in late life enjoyed sitting on her veranda at Turriell Point remembering the area from when she was young, the sandy reach covered with grass, pigeon-berry vine and oak trees. There was a pasture yard for cattle with a stockyard used for the mustering of the family cattle. When the timber was cut from the water's edge the sandbank started moving. This area is the Deeban Spit.

The pioneering life was hard, particularly for the women. There was the loneliness of the bush, the heat of summer and cold winters in simple slab huts with few amenities, the frightening sound of a dingo's howl in the night or a sick baby whimpering. They bore and raised large families in an era when more women died of complications during childbirth than from any other cause. Some, in time, acquired a comfortable home but many struggled all their lives.

Thomas Mitchell and the Old Illawarra Road

Thomas Livingstone Mitchell (1792-1855) was the son of John Mitchell and his wife Janet Wilson of Craigend, Scotland. His working career began when he was employed in an uncle's colliery when he was 17 years. By June 1811 he was gazetted a second lieutenant in the 95th Regiment of Foot. It was the time of the Peninsular War and the regiment was one of the Duke of Wellington's Light Division. Mitchell spent much of his time surveying, mapping and in topographical intelligence work and established a reputation as a surveyor and draughtsman.

By 1826 he had risen to the rank of major and the following year was offered "3 difft. Situations at New South Wales worth £500 a year each – a Collector, Civil Engineer and a second, or assist., to Mr [John] Oxley with the reversion of his appt."

Mitchell chose to be assistant to Mr Oxley and in September 1827 arrived in Sydney to assume the position of deputy surveyor general. He was accompanied by his wife, Mary, daughter of General Blunt, and their children. Mitchell was involved in map making, road surveying and the collation of numerous detached surveys, to form a general map of the colony. Oxley died in May 1828 and Mitchell was appointed surveyor general. He surveyed eastern Australia, laid out towns, roads, public reserves and personally surveyed the main southern and western roads.

Settlement of the Illawarra district on the south coast began in 1815 but by the 1840s was still reliant on shipping to carry produce and supplies to and from Sydney. The only road was by way of Liverpool, Campbelltown and Appin. Pioneer Charles Throsby had hacked a rough track in 1815 to give access to water and grass for his cattle on the Illawarra plain which Governor Macquarie travelled along in 1822. Macquarie found the road through Airds and Appin "tolerably good" for the first 20 miles but the rest of the way to the Mountain Pass of Illawarra "is the most execrably bad for any sort of wheel-carriage. This very bad road commences at

King's Falls, where we crossed the head of George's River near its source".

Conditions deteriorated and on 15 January the party put the luggage on three pack horses to continue. They crossed the Cataract River near its source and arrived at the summit "of the great mountain that contains the pass to the low country of Illawarra". The governor found the descent "very rugged, rocky, and slippery, and so many obstacles opposed themselves to our progress, that it was with great difficulty that the pack-horses could get down this horrid steep descent".

By 1831 Major Mitchell decided that a more direct line of road should be built from the Illawarra to Sydney, more or less parallel to the coastline. He was influenced by "a very able survey of the intervening country" made by Assistant Surveyor Govett. He suggested to the colonial secretary the road should cross the lowest ford on Cooks River and the Georges River by a ferry "across a breadth of two hundred and fifty yards". Mitchell checked the route himself but chose his son, Roderick, the assistant surveyor to make the exact survey. Mitchell believed the mail cart from Wollongong to Sydney would travel by a route 20 miles shorter than the old route via Appin. The road was duly mapped out and constructed between 1843 and 1845.

On early maps the new Illawarra Road was referred to as "Sir Thomas Mitchell's Line of Road to the Illawarra" and sometimes called the Wollongong Road. It began south of Cooks River dam, went through Arncliffe and followed the ridge of today's Forest Road, to the Georges River at Lugarno and the heights of Menai. It then skirted the tidal waters of the Woronora River but passed over the river at the ford, and onto Heathcote, Mt Keira and

Thomas Livingstone Mitchell (1792-1855), surveyor general, surveyed the Old Illawarra Road in 1843. This was the first surveyed road in what is now Sutherland Shire and was primarily designed as a route from Sydney to the Illawarra. The causeway where this road crossed the Woronora River can still be seen on the upper reaches of the river. (Sydney Illustrated News, 13 May 1854, Mitchell Library)

the Illawarra. Mitchell reported to the colonial secretary "such a course will not cross a single watercourse between the head of navigation of Woronora and the point of Bulli".

A road-gang of ten convicts under Overseer O'Hara worked on the Illawarra Road, the only time convicts were used in the Sutherland area. Transportation of convicts to New South Wales ceased in 1840.

Thomas Cook, a convict, who worked on the Great Western Road road-gang to Bathurst wrote "With a sheet of Bark for my bed, the half of a threadbare Blanket for my covering, and a Log for my pillow … and many a tear did I shed, when contemplating upon my hard fate".

During the Macquarie era, as Robert Hughes in *The Fatal Shore* points out, Commissioner Bigge, who was sent to investigate the colony, believed convicts at gang labour should get no initiative and work only at such uniform tasks as grubbing out the giant roots of gum trees left in the ground by earlier clearing parties. Mitchell warned of the extreme roughness of the district and against allowing men to stray too far from camp. He also gave instructions as to where the convict huts were to be fixed, near trees Mitchell had marked.

By June 1843 Assistant Superintendent Darke was working "in the Georges River locality" and directed to take charge of the survey and camp as near as possible to the Woronora crossing. Mitchell also wanted him appointed a district magistrate to enforce discipline. Roderick Mitchell at the same time was instructed to survey the Woronora River "downwards".

In May 1844 it was reported one of the party, in endeavouring to obtain a hearth-stone for his hut, fell over a cliff and was "dashed from rock to rock" but his body was not found. Mitchell suspected foul play and ordered a full enquiry. The same month Overseer O'Hara was dismissed for not having sufficient control over his men. Darke and his party surveyed and cleared the line of the road but the road building was done by contract. By May 1845 Assistant Superintendent Darke had reached Bulli. Darke later became a Town Surveyor in Sydney and is remembered in Darkes Forest.

Mitchell's plan was to have a low level bridge constructed across the Georges River at Lugarno but to save costs this plan was abandoned. A punt service began operations on 6 February 1843. The Lugarno punt ceased operations in 1864 and the service was not resumed until 1887. Nevertheless, when the Lugarno ferry ceased operations on 12 December 1974 it was the oldest continuing ferry service in New South Wales. From the punt, Mitchell's road then crossed the Menai Ridge, decreasing the route to the south coast by 20 miles.

In 1924 Cridland, in his book on Sutherland Shire, noted of the road to the ford on the Woronora River, past:

the newly christened village of Engadine that some thirty five years ago the unemployed of the day were engaged in reconstructing this latter portion on quite an ambitious scale. The old track, which here wound round the face of a steep hill, was widened to a broad carriage-way forty feet across by blasting the stone out of the hill on the upper side, packing the centre, and building a retaining embankment to the lower edge. This embankment in places rises to a height of over forty feet.

He noted the reconditioned road stopped short of the river but recommenced "some distance back in the hills on the other side of the ford … originally there was a stone weir across the river, but storms have long since washed away almost every trace of it". Mitchell named the ford on the Woronora the Pass of Sabugal after a town in Portugal where Wellington's troops fought during the Peninsular War. When the punt was established at Tom Uglys in 1863 the road between Lugarno and Heathcote was seldom used. Mitchell won fame as an explorer and also published a variety of literary works. He was said to be difficult to work with and both Governors Bourke and Darling found him impossible to manage. Explorers Sturt and Gregory complained of his "gratuitous rudeness and lack of co-operation".

Mitchell was predeceased by his second son, Roderick, who mapped the Barwon River and led an expedition to search for Leichhardt's missing party. While voyaging from Moreton Bay to Sydney, he fell overboard from the ship and was drowned on 28 August 1851. Mitchell received a knighthood but his last years were clouded by an inquiry into his department which criticised defects in organisation and procedure. Mitchell died on 5 October 1855 and was survived by his wife, Mary and four of their 12 children.

The Illawarra Railway

The Sydney Railway Company was incorporated on 10 October 1849 by Act of parliament. The turning of the first sod was carried out by Mrs K Stewart, a daughter of the Governor, Sir Charles Fitzroy on 3 July 1850 for a proposed link from Sydney to Goulburn. Thomas Holt was a director of the Sydney Tramway and Railway Company in 1850 after he proposed the then director, Charles Cowper (1807-1875) resign as chairman but remain as a manager. Cowper, who later became a premier of New South Wales, was an advocate of railway construction. Generally the early Australian railways followed the English methods but there was also an American influence. Initially, heavy rails of the English type were used but, as these were costly, they were replaced with lighter ones. The eucalypt forests of the coastal areas provided track sleepers. An American method of fastening the rails directly to them by spikes was followed, rather than the English method of setting them in chairs.

By the 1870s there was agitation for improved and increased railway services for the metropolitan area of Sydney. On the booming south coast transport was by sea, or Mitchell's Illawarra Road, but both methods of transport were inadequate for the coal, iron ore, kerosene shale and farm products being transported.

In 1872 the South Coast Railway Committee was formed and one company planned to build a narrow gauge link to the south coast. Several surveys began in the 1800s and coal companies wanted the line to terminate at Balmain where shipping facilities could be constructed. Landholders and speculators lobbied the Minister for Public Works, John Sutherland. Sutherland was an enthusiast for the railway and realised that, to open up the Port Hacking district, the railway should extend across the Georges River to the Illawarra.

John Whitton (1820-1898) had been appointed engineer-in-chief of the New South Wales Railways in 1857 and served for 32 years, pioneering the famous zig-zag railway and he commissioned a survey in 1873. The survey followed the proposed narrow gauge railway but, as coal was evident around the Hacking River, a diversion would be needed for new collieries.

However, in 1879 the Premier, Sir John Robertson, dedicated the area of National Park covering 16,000 acres and thwarted the proposed coal interests. Thomas Holt was one who hoped to profit from coal but it did not prove viable. The railway line was to have traversed a portion of Holt's property but Holt demanded compensation of £1,547.10.0 for 3 acres, 3 roods and 32 perches at Sylvania which he had bought as Crown land for £1 per acre. The government

Sutherland railway station in 1887. The opening of the Illawarra line to Sutherland in 1885 helped create a township in this quiet bush setting. The first subdivision and sale of land was held here in 1886 and by the end of the decade there were about 50 families resident. (SPF, Mitchell Library)

was outraged and accepted an offer from other property owners who promised free access for construction purposes. Plans were made for the railway to extend from Hurstville and cross the Georges River at Como.

Whitton's survey was not completed until 1875, the line to commence at Balmain, where deep water shipping facilities would be built, under the western railway at Petersham, via Dulwich Hill to Tempe and onto Rocky Point.

It was proposed there would be a rail crossing at Sans Souci, an ascent of the "Goumea" range, following the western shore of Hacking Creek and on to Otford where a tunnel would lead the railway on to the coast at Stanwell Park and Coalcliff. Another tunnel would take the railway to Bulli and Wollongong, and the coal mines. This survey cost £2,547 but it was found Rocky Point was unsuitable as a crossing. Although the river was shallower here it was difficult to obtain

foundations for bridge piers, and it was then decided to make a crossing at Como. In 1881 John Whitton reported the three surveyors of the railway had made a final survey:

the centre line to be staked from the junction with the southern railway between Eveleigh and Macdonaldtown platforms, to Georges River; thence via the ridge on which the Bottle Forest Road had been formed to a point 14 miles north of Bulli Pass.

Sutherland station undergoing reconstruction for the new branch line to Cronulla, in December 1939. This railway extension, the last major rail construction in Sydney until the 1980s, necessitated major changes to Sutherland station. (Australian Railway Historical Society, NSW Division Archives)

Sutherland railway station and the small Sutherland township, 1890. In the foreground work proceeds on the duplication of the railway line to the Illawarra district. From the 1880s to the 1930s work on building or extending railways was a ready source of employment for labourers. (Mitchell Library)

Valley, although the Bottle Forest route was found less expensive and was upheld after an inquiry. The construction company had ceased work at today's Sutherland Station and when advised to recommence, the workers declined to proceed. The work was abandoned at the site of the Como Railway Station but the contractors eventually won £20,000 for breach of contract. In July 1884 a new contract was awarded to Messrs Rowe & Smith. On 15 October 1884 the double track to Hurstville was officially opened. There was a brick platform and a building on the eastern side of the line.

Beyond Hurstville there was a single line to Penshurst, Mortdale, Oatley, Como, Sutherland, Loftus Junction and Heathcote. The line Hurstville to Sutherland was officially opened on 26 December 1885 but there were not regular

In the same year the Public Works Act authorised the raising of £1,020,000 for the railway from Sydney to Wollongong and Kiama. In 1882 tenders were called for the first section, some 23 miles, 13 chains, to Waterfall.

The tender for the work went to the lowest priced of the tenders, C & E Miller & Co, and included the construction of a bridge across the Georges River at Como. Construction camps were established at Tempe and Como. A large shanty town grew on the heights of Como, a wooden Woniora Hotel opened, and a German Club was formed by the many German railway workers and fishermen along the Georges River. The club later became the Como Hotel. The work of the railway did not proceed without conflict as the colonial secretary questioned the Bottle Forest route, favouring the Hacking River

The Nowra mail train at Sutherland station, late 1880s. Well-dressed local children sit placidly on the western side of the station. There are, by this time, a number of substantial buildings, including the Railway Hotel (on left), east of the station. (Mitchell Library)

services as the Como Bridge had not been tested at the time. Como Bridge was completed in September 1885 but was not to be used until the line to Waterfall was completed. However, excursion trains operated to Sutherland from 26 December until 4 January 1886, before the bridge was fully tested. Tests using three tender-type locomotives were singly driven over the bridge, then coupled and crossed at 25 mph. The test satisfied the inspecting engineers with a maximum deflection of only ¾ inch.

The lattice girder type bridge was 956 feet long with four main girders, and cross girders carried longitudinal girders to support the single rail track. In 1972 the single-track bridge was replaced by a double-track one but the earlier bridge survived. Its ownership was transferred to the Metropolitan Water Board as, since 1942,

Tram driver Andrew Harvey and conductor Edward Howard pose with the last passenger tram to run between Sutherland and Cronulla on 3 August 1931. The goods service terminated a few months later. (Australian Railway Historical Society, NSW Division Archives)

The Illawarra rail line crossing the Georges River, from the Sydney Illustrated News, 16 January 1886. *This sketch shows the northern approaches to this historic steel truss construction which carried the railway line until 1972. It was replaced by a double-track bridge and now serves as a cycle and walkway. (Mitchell Library)*

the bridge had carried the Woronora water pipeline over the Georges River. In 1985 the old bridge became a cycleway and walkway from the former Como Pleasure Grounds to Oatley shopping area.

The line to Waterfall opened on 9 March 1886 and had a branch line to Loftus. The locomotives obtained water, pumped from Lake Engadine, just before Bottle Forest overbridge. There was duplication of the line to Waterfall in 1890, and the station relocated north of the original site. A turntable was installed and from 1905 there were improved facilities at Waterfall.

Originally 16 terminating trains operated to Hurstville daily with two services to Sutherland and two more to Waterfall. In 1884 through services started to Kiama with two passenger services and one mixed service daily. There were three additional suburban trains to Como, three to Sutherland and one to Waterfall. At weekends there were additional services to National Park. The single track from Hurstville was duplicated in 1899 because of demands of traffic but a bottleneck resulted at Como and remained a problem until November 1972.

The arrival of the railway changed the way of life for the Sutherland area. Weekend picnic parties were attracted to Como and pleasure gardens opened. From Sutherland station a road led to Cronulla beaches and visitors arrived at Loftus Junction to visit National Park.

Coaches, Buses and Steam Trams

When the Illawarra railway forged through to Sutherland the surrounding countryside was still mostly bush with settlement around the shores of the Georges River and Port Hacking. Roads, merely bush tracks, developed linking the new railway station at Sutherland and, with time, areas such as Sylvania, Caringbah, Cronulla and Gymea developed. Some of Sydney's wealthier residents established weekenders on the headlands on the shores of the Georges River and Port Hacking. Their only access was by horse or by the waterways.

Frank Cridland in his *Port Hacking, Cronulla and Sutherland Shire* talks of the romance of the early days of travel in the area. Port Hacking was then a 20 mile run from Sydney and "Saturday afternoon always saw a procession of well-groomed horses and stylish vehicles making their way along the road from Sydney." Cridland states the distance was "a fine trying-out ground on which to test a promising horse, or bring up to his paces a half-broken colt". He divided the owners of the horses into two classes, one "composed of men who drove sedately and never extended their quiet, well-broken horses; the other of the more 'sporty' fellows who possessed

Two Sutherland and Cronulla Beach coaches outside Giddings store and post office. Albert and Agnes Giddings ran a well-patronised coach service between Sutherland station and Cronulla Beach until the opening of the Sutherland-Cronulla tramline in 1911. Their store and post office agency on the corner of Gerrale Street and Nicholson Parade was constructed in 1900 and extended in 1910. (Cronulla Surf Club)

the fastest horses they could secure, and were always ready for a challenge to a speed contest."

Some of the best horses were seen on the Sydney to Port Hacking trail and men with weekend blocks on the bay owned some of the fastest horses. Even after the advent of the train "about a dozen Sydney carriers" still drove their own turnouts to their weekenders on parts of Port Hacking. On one occasion, however, a group decided to hire the biggest and best drag in Sydney, pulled by five horses and driven by a competent driver. They all enjoyed a successful day and made sure the driver remained sober for the return journey. Unfortunately, in the darkness of night on the return trip, on the Lilli Pilli Road he turned the drag over, smashing it beyond repair, and tipped his 25 male passengers "into the bush in all directions from the tallest vehicle in Sydney". Although bruised and shaken none were injured.

Once the railway arrived at Sutherland an era of coaches followed. The Giddings family established a coach service (c. 1895) from the station to Cronulla and at one time had five coaches and 56 horses. From 1906 the firm carried the mail between Sutherland and Cronulla and the same year appealed to the new Sutherland Shire to prevent William Burgess, a Kogarah – Sylvania coachman, from running his coach service to Cronulla in competition with Giddings. Coach services were numerous. Others operated from Sutherland to Yowie Bay, Kogarah to Sylvania, and Lilli Pilli via Port Hacking

Hunter's "Rockdale and Cronulla via Taren Point and Port Hacking Road" motor service. J S Hunter advertised this service which began operating in 1916, with the slogan "Surfing made easy". These early buses used the recently opened punt service at Taren Point, a considerably shorter route than the alternative of crossing the Georges River at Tom Uglys Point. (GPO, Mitchell Library)

Road. The proprietor of a Port Hacking coach line, named Parker, found it profitable to sell his coach line and purchased a blacksmith's at Miranda which he enlarged to repair and paint the many horse coaches in the shire.

Most remarkably, a woman also operated a passenger service from 1907. Sarah Stork began with a sulky and graduated to a five horse and passenger coach when the Waterfall Hospital for Consumptives (later Garrawarra Hospital, 1958-1991) was established in 1909. The coach was replaced with a converted truck around 1918 and later an International truck called "Old Biddie". Another pioneer was Daniel Lobb of Otford who operated a coach service from Loftus Junction to Audley at National Park. Until the railway arrived at Engadine in 1920, a hackney coach operated from the district to Heathcote. This was owned by a man named Cooper, who originally was contracted to the Railways Department to cut wood for the steam trains. Cooper met each train and charged his passengers by the week. A two passenger horse coach was operated by a Menai resident, William Mackin, which normally crossed the Georges River by the Lugarno ferry. On one occasion his horses bolted and the coach and the two passengers ended up in the river.

The local school children also often travelled by horse bus. The first school bus from Sylvania to Miranda Central was driven by Charlie Butterfield and early photographs have captured the students posing in and around this horse drawn vehicle.

Following the 1890s depression, development slowed but by the early 1900s progress in the form of motor buses and steam trams arrived in the Sutherland area. The first motor bus, capable of seating 19 passengers, made its appearance in 1908 and operated between Sutherland and Cronulla. The bus had a 45 hp engine and took 20 minutes for the trip at a cost of eight pence a passenger. The same year the steam tramway between Sutherland and Cronulla was approved, but the service did not begin until 12 June 1911. A motor bus service began from Kogarah to Sylvania in 1912 and two years later another bus was given council permission to operate from Sutherland to Gymea Bay. Two charabancs (from the French "carriage with seats"), or motor coaches, began a service from Loftus Junction to Audley in 1914, operated by Ned Toyer, and in 1915 extended to Sutherland.

In 1911 Sutherland had a population of 2,896 which climbed to 7,705 by 1921 and by the early 1920s there were bus services between Cronulla and Port Hacking, Sylvania and Cronulla, Taren Point and Lilli Pilli, and Caringbah and the headwaters of Dolans Bay. Fred Bardsley had commenced services between Cronulla and Sydney, and Cronulla to Hurstville in the 1920s. He used imported buses from the USA and his drivers wore white coats and caps. Bardsley also operated Studebaker cars and in 1929 imported the first of three Leyland double decker buses which he painted blue and started with a crank handle. The buses also carried the mail bags. In the 1930s the government stopped private bus services in the city.

The attraction of the surfing beach at Cronulla resulted in the construction of a tramway from Sutherland to Cronulla. Before the steam tram could begin operations from Sutherland, provision had to be made for an ample supply of water for the tram and the Sydney Water Board constructed a six inch pipeline from Penshurst to Miranda. Those with properties along the pipeline were allowed to tap into the pipe and use the water but, of course, they were rated. Work on the tramway was quicker than the building of the pipeline.

On 12 June 1911 the first tram left Sutherland for Cronulla at 5.56 am, then headed back to Sutherland at 7.15 am. An official opening was celebrated on 26 June the same year.

The construction work was carried out by George Gilmore and the tramway covered 7 miles 32 chains. It carried both passengers and freight, taking about 35 minutes for the journey. The line ran along the Princes Highway in a northerly direction to the council chambers, then followed a separate right-of-way in an easterly direction south of the highway. It continued along the southern side of Kingsway to the Port Hacking Road intersection, and south along the centre of Curranulla Street (later Cronulla Street), east along Waratah Street and south along Ewos Parade to a loop near Shelly Beach in Shelly Park. Terminal sheds for the tramway were south of the present Sutherland Railway Station and, as the tram was a single track line, there was a reversing loop behind the down platform at Sutherland Station. In addition there were crossing loops at Acacia Road, Miranda, Caringbah and Woolooware Roads. Goods sidings were located into Sutherland brick works, at Miranda, at Caringbah, at Woolooware Road and at

Curranulla Street, Cronulla. In addition two storage sidings were provided at Cronulla terminus. All that survives of the Sutherland – Cronulla tramway are two relocated waiting sheds and a brick passenger shed, and ticket office which in recent times has been used as the office of a real estate agent.

There were four tramway motors, with eight cars. On week days one motor and car operated, with an additional motor and car at peak periods, and passenger trams ran every two hours. The goods tram, of a dummy truck and three railway trucks, ran as required but usually twice daily. It was estimated the line carried up to 2,000 tons of freight every three months. However, on weekends and holidays three motors, and from three to six cars, were used for the passengers. It was reported that during the Easter holidays of 1912 some 12,340 people used the tram service.

The attractions of Cronulla and the beach were so popular that by 1914, on the eve of World I, the tramway had five motors and 11 cars as stock, one car capable of carrying 60 passengers. The residential area of Cronulla and Miranda increased and by 1924 three motors and nine cars were in regular daily service and on Sundays four motors and eight cars.

In 1926 an electric rail service operated from St James in the city to Sutherland and the tram then ran an hourly service on week days. With the era of the car gaining popularity in the late 1920s, the tram passengers declined and due, it was said, to bad management and a rival motor bus service, the steam tram ceased operations on 3 August 1931. The goods service operated until 12 February 1932 when it too ceased operations

and the line closed. In 1965 one of the tram's waiting sheds from Miranda went to the Tramway Museum at Loftus and another from Cronulla is now a waiting shed on Cronulla public wharf. In the days of the tram service the sheds were lit by kerosene lamps but these were frequently stolen.

In 1911 Cronulla was declared an urban area and the steam tram, despite the use of the outdated rolling stock on occasions, served the community until its demise.

The Waterways, Paddle Wheelers and Ferries

Sutherland Shire is surrounded by fine waterways and, in early days, water transport was often the only means of access to some isolated areas. Following the construction of Mitchell's Illawarra Road, a crossing for the Georges River was required. The contract for the operation of a hand punt over the river was won by Charles Roman who commenced operations in 1843, the beginning of the Lugarno ferry service.

Three brothers, named Sanbrook, who were building contractors in Camperdown, began operating paddle wheelers on the Georges River in the 1890s. The service ran from a wharf

Max Hinder photograph of "Audrey and friends" relaxing at Port Hacking, 1922. (GPO, Mitchell Library)

The opening of Cronulla Ocean Wharf at Salmon Haul Reserve, South Cronulla on 26 January 1919 was a well attended function. Returned soldiers, scouts, members of the South Cronulla Progress Association and writer Henry Lawson are among the crowd who watched the governor of New South Wales, Sir Walter Davidson, cut the ribbon. The cost of construction was shared by the North Coast Steam Navigation Company and the shire council. John Hill (on the extreme left) shire president and local boat builder, was credited with being largely responsible for the project which aimed to bring tourists from Sydney to Cronulla by boat. (Descendants of John Hill)

adjacent to the southern end of the Como Railway Bridge to Parkesvale. This popular picnic resort was the inspiration of the brothers and named for the son of Sir Henry Parkes, Varney Parkes who was the member of parliament for Canterbury. (Parkes' first wife was Clarinda Varney). In 1900 Varney Parkes was the guest-of-honour at the official opening of the river service to Parkesvale.

The paddle wheel excursions proved popular and the Sanbrooks also offered an evening cruise by moonlight. Combined rail – steamer tickets were available at the cost of two shillings and sixpence first class, or one shilling and sixpence second class. On occasions a photographer named Davis travelled on the vessels taking photographs and selling ice cream. Passengers enjoyed the excursions which also called at Lugarno Reserve, and residents of Menai (originally Bangor) made good use of the service.

In 1899 Thomas Jack Price, the first permanent settler on the Woronora River provided a rowboat service for locals and travellers to cross the river and follow the rough track to the infant Sutherland and the Illawarra railway. The track became known as Prices Track. Price charged each passenger threepence for the crossing and was assisted by an elderly man named Quaife, affectionately called "Old Ned".

It was in the 1890s that the old hand winched punt at Lugarno was replaced with a larger punt but there were constant complaints about the 30 minute crossing time of the river. A crossing could be exciting such as the time when the cable broke and punt and passengers drifted upstream. On occasions, when the punt broke down, once for six weeks, market gardeners had to revert to taking their produce, via Sutherland, to the Tom Uglys punt.

Hurstville council steadfastly refused to man the punt after daylight hours. By 1917 residents

A group of picnickers look down at Cronulla Ocean Wharf from Salmon Haul Reserve, 1922. Use of this wharf was intermittent. Excursion boats, deterred by heavy swells and the wharf's exposed position, often returned to Sydney without stopping. By 1924 the service was discontinued and the wharf was later dismantled. (GPO, Mitchell Library)

were calling for the punt to become steam driven and to be nationalised. Remuneration for the ferrymen was not excessive, "Dad" Saunders, a ferryman, received only £2 a week for his long hours of duty. From 1922 Sutherland Shire Council assumed control of the ferry and in 1928 it became a six car motor ferry.

With the increase in traffic over the years, the ferry became inadequate and many were the complaints about the long queues forced to wait to board the ferry.

Even in 1961, when a new 16 car ferry was introduced, the queues of traffic continued. In 1973 the new concrete bridge was constructed to span the river from Alfords Point Road and relieve some of the traffic congestion.

It is claimed the first punt at the famous Tom Uglys crossing was operated by an old soldier named Tom, in 1863. One origin for the place name is that Tom had a wooden leg and was known as "Tom Wooden-leg" which the local Aborigines corrupted to "Tom Woggley", which became "Tom Ogly", then "Tom Ugly".

Although the true origin of the name is unknown, it has also been said to be an Aboriginal corruption of Tom Huxley.

In 1864 William Harris began a hand operated punt across to Horse Rock Point, Sylvania. His income was derived only from the passengers' fares and he had to obtain permission to journey through Thomas Holt's estate. The punt was later replaced and by 1888 the first steam ferry began operations. Tom Uglys was a popular crossing and in the early 1900s it was estimated some "200 vehicles and 225 horses" per day used the ferry. The service was popular

with the local market gardeners who had to carry their produce to Sydney.

By 1910 an additional ferry was operating but again long lines of traffic often waited for the ferry. Even when a modern 30 car ferry was introduced in 1922 holiday crowds waited on each side of the crossing. Steam ferries continued the service until the Georges River Bridge opened in April 1929. This bridge served the local communities until the new bridge opened in October 1987.

Punts and ferries are part of the history of Sutherland Shire and in 1914 an order was placed for the construction of a steam ferry to run from Taren Point to Rocky Point, Sans Souci. The service began on 18 March 1916. Again the service proved popular and from 18 March to 31 August 1916 the ferry carried 559 motor cycles, 3,974 cars and trucks, and 6,308 horse drawn vehicles. In 1954 an older, but larger punt built in 1921, was put into service, capable of carrying 26 vehicles. In its last years of service it averaged 1,000 cars a day.

In 1962 tenders were called for the construction of a bridge. The tender was awarded to John Holland (Constructions) Pty Ltd, with the bridge designed by the Department of Main Roads. The bridge took three years to construct at a cost of $3,000 and was 1,560 feet long. It was officially opened by the Governor of New South Wales, Sir Eric Woodward, on 29 May 1965. With the completion of the Captain Cook Bridge the old ferry was no longer required and ceased service on 27 May 1965.

Before the World War I, the North Coast Steam Navigation Company had excursions to

Port Hacking and a wharf was built in the area adjacent to Hungry Point at South Cronulla. Excursions operated from Sussex Street in the city to Cronulla, a round trip of 30 miles. This leisurely trip south along the coast, past the beaches of Bondi and Coogee, was popular with residents of South Cronulla. Passengers, men in suits and women in long skirts and wide shady hats, enjoyed the thrill of the sea excursion but when the service halted in 1924 it appeared the company had made no profit from the popular outings.

The National Park soon attracted visitors who wished to enjoy the attractions of this newly preserved natural bush area. *The South Coast Illustrated Tourists' Guide*, published in 1924, states "The launch excursion between Gunnamatta Bay [Cronulla] and Audley [National Park] is superb, and presents ever changing views of a veritable fairyland of waters and foliage". A ferry service operated from 1909 to Audley from Cronulla.

The little holiday resort of Bundeena, which Cridland in 1924 said "threatens to become a struggletown", soon acquired a passenger service from Gunnamatta Bay. The service began in 1916 and was operated by Mrs Kingham of Simpson's Hotel, Bundeena. The *Myanbla* ferry, operated by an ex-square rigger seaman, Captain Ryall, also became a familiar sight on Gunnamatta Bay. The captain retired to Tuross Heads on the south coast but the ferry was the pioneer of the larger ferries that soon followed.

Time, progress and the increase in road traffic meant the death-knell of the picturesque old punts and ferries of Sutherland Shire.

Como Pleasure Grounds and Como Hotel

Sutherland Shire has many fine parks and recreational areas. One of the earliest and historically important is the Como Pleasure Grounds.

James Murphy who bored for coal on Thomas Holt's Sutherland estate and was a promoter of the first Holt-Sutherland Estate Co, founded and named Como. It is believed to have been named because of a similarity with Lake Como, Italy. On the western side of Como Railway Station Murphy built Como House, an alpine style timber residence which, after his death, became a popular boarding house. By 1969 it was vacant and partially burnt down, then demolished and the land subdivided. Murphy also established the Como Pleasure Grounds on the Georges River c. 1888 just a few years after the arrival of the Illawarra railway. Here he created terraced garden walks with small summer houses with picnic tables, a swimming pool, boat shed, communal pavilion and dance hall and, on the summit of the property, a large garden house with views over the bushland and river.

From the early 1890s paddle wheelers operated along the Georges River from a wharf adjacent to the southern end of Como railway bridge and they enjoyed great popularity. One

was the *Telephone*, built in 1878, and once used by the Balmain Ferry Company in Sydney. It travelled the river as far as Parkesvale, opposite Picnic Point. Boats could be hired at the Como Boatsheds, one operated by J H Wills, and the fishing was good on the Georges River. Behind a boatshed stood a small wooden cottage built by Murphy for an employee, William Jordan, who cared for the rowboats. Murphy also established a little general store to serve the holiday-makers who walked from the railway, by a pathway, to the Como Hotel. At one time the store was operated by George Rollings and his wife who had arrived at Como in the early 1900s. Rollings had operated a boarding house in the old Woniora Hotel.

Writer D.H. Lawrence and his wife, Frieda, arrived in Sydney on 27 May 1922 on the P & O ship *Malwa*. A few days later they travelled by train south to a bungalow, Wyewurk, at Thirroul where Lawrence worked on the first draft of novel *Kangaroo*, in which he writes:

'Como', said the station sign. And they ran on the bridges over two arms of water from the sea, and they saw what looked like a long lake with wooded shores and bungalows: a bit like Lake Como, but oh, so unlike. That curious sombreness of Australia, the sense of oldness, with the forms all worn down low and blunt squat. The squat-seeming earth.

Como Bridge with the pleasure gardens in the distance. The house on the right is probably Como House erected by James Murphy in about 1886. This has been described by local historian Verena Morton as a "most ornate two-storeyed weatherboard house ... similar in design to an alpine timbered house." (Mitchell Library)

Como on the Georges River, photographed by Charles Kerry. James Murphy, the manager of the Holt-Sutherland Estate, developed Como Pleasure Grounds in the late 1880s on this promontory, located near Como Hotel. This was, for about 20 years, a popular picnic and leisure spot for people arriving on the train and alighting at Como station. Some clearing and landscaping had been undertaken when this photo was taken. (GPO, Mitchell Library)

One of the large construction camps for the building of the Illawarra railway was at Como, then called Woniora. Among the construction men were German settlers and the famous Como Hotel was initially built as a German club for these workers, or some say as a social club for the German Consul, or the Concordia Club of Sydney. M. Hutton Neve in *A Short Authentic History of Cronulla* states the hotel was said to have been built by a Frenchman, M. Porcham but pointed out others say it was built by a German. The earliest licensee is reputed to be Sidney Staples but in 1909 Paul Buchholz is credited with converting the building to an hotel. Buchholz was succeeded as licensee by a Mr Paton. Many of the men had their families living at the railway camp and a timber portable school was built for the children which opened in February 1884 and overlooked Scylla and Double Bays. It was only a temporary measure and when the railway was completed the school closed in 1885. The present Como School stands on the site of this temporary one but dates from 1921.

The construction camp later moved to Heathcote and the Woniora Hotel, originally built of wattlebark and hessian, served the workers and weekend fishermen until it closed and its licence transferred to Heathcote. The German Club then became the Como Hotel. The building was dated at c. 1880 and was certainly completed before 1883. It was built of timber and brick covered with stucco and had a distinctive central square tower. The hotel overlooked Scylla Bay, but in the 1930s the bay was reclaimed and used as a football field.

The hotel was one of the few remaining 19th century buildings in the shire. Many of the visitors to the Como Pleasure Gardens rowed to the famous hotel and the writer Henry Lawson often visited the hotel in the years before his death in 1922. He is said to have traded his poems for drinks at the hotel.

In 1954 it was proposed Sutherland Shire Council buy the hotel for use as a community centre but the owners, Tooth & Co, refused to sell. In more recent times it was owned by former rugby league star Arthur Beetson. In 1989 the first floor was an Italian restaurant and later a seafood restaurant. In 1977 the building was listed by the National Trust of Australia (NSW). Tragically in the early hours of Sunday, 3 November 1996 the old historic hotel was destroyed by fire. The owners, John Mead and Mike O'Connor, plan to rebuild the hotel on the same site, replicating the style.

The Como Pleasure Grounds survive jutting into the Georges River in the shadow of the railway bridge. There are old fig trees and landscaped areas with barbeque facilities and playground equipment where an earlier generation enjoyed riverside picnics.

This photograph, c. 1886, shows the German Club (later Como Hotel), unfenced and with no landscaping, overlooking Scylla Bay (now Scylla Bay Oval). Como Hotel, a distinctive local feature, was destroyed by fire in 1996. Although the railway bridge had been constructed when this photo was taken there are few signs of the later development that would take place in this locality. (SPF, Mitchell Library)

The Shire of Sutherland

Sutherland Shire was proclaimed in the *Government Gazette* of 7 March 1906 and the provisional council met at the Miranda School of Arts on 18 June the same year. W C Danne was appointed as the provisional shire clerk and received 30 shillings a week.

The first elections were held on 5 December 1906 and council held their first meeting that month. The council consisted of seven councillors: R W Cook, John Hill, E W Hyndman, W G Judd, Thomas Lehane, C M McAlister, and J W MacFarlane who was appointed shire clerk.

The prominent businessman, W G Judd, became the first shire president and held the position until 1910 when he was succeeded by Councillor W E Hyndman, 1911-1915. The residents of Sutherland Shire numbered 1,500 in 1906, but only ratepayers were eligible to vote. Within a mile of Sutherland were some 90 houses and ten places of business. The shire was divided into three ridings, A, B and C and the western boundary was west to Bangor (later called Menai).

Within the shire were many commercial fishermen, market gardens, orchards and poultry farms. Frank Cridland in *Port Hacking, Cronulla and Sutherland Shire* light-heartedly suggests chicken should have been incorporated into the shire's coat of arms as they were so prolific.

From 1906 the new council met in a simple shop, built of brick with a wooden veranda and residence at the rear, in Railway Parade (818-820 Princes Highway), Sutherland, between Boyle Street and President Avenue. The building was rented for 15 shillings a week and the shire clerk paid five shillings a week for use of the rear residence. This building was used until 1915. In 1909 the Holt-Sutherland Estate donated land at the corner of the Princes Highway and Eton Street for new council premises. The council moved to the new two storeyed council chambers in 1915 which was extended in 1928. It was demolished when council occupied the Sutherland Council Administration Centre, opened in 1964. Major alterations were made to that building in the mid 1970s.

Following Federation all the Australian states overhauled the system of local government. In 1905 New South Wales passed a shires Act and consolidated its system in 1906. It is said that in Australia there is nothing to correspond with the hierarchial organisation of local government found in Britain. The Local Government (Shires) Act of 1905 provided that the whole of the State (there were certain exceptions) be divided into shires and named by the governor of New South Wales. Accordingly the governor, Admiral Sir Harry Holdsworth Rawson (1902-1909), selected the name Sutherland, proclaimed the district as Sutherland, No. 133 (the 133rd District) and fixed the boundaries.

The new Sutherland Shire Council of 1906 called for preservation of the foreshores of Botany Bay, Port Hacking and the beaches of the shire. In the early days the council chambers in Sutherland were somewhat isolated from many of the shire residents as there was no network of auxiliary roads, except perhaps rough tracks, to Como, Menai, Grays Point, North-West Arm, Kurnell and Bundeena. From 1 January 1907 Sutherland Shire Council assumed responsibility for the shire's roads and bridges but, with a small income, the provision of adequate roads was an early problem.

In an area with much natural bushland not only the roads, but also water services, reserves and parks were reclaimed from virgin bush. One of council's first purchases from the State government was a supply of muck-picks, adzes, rock-picks and spalling hammers.

The council was short of funds and councillor McAlister erected and maintained at his own expense a street lamp in Gerrale Street, Cronulla. There was elation when approval was given in 1908 for the building of the Sutherland – Cronulla tramway which would bring more visitors to the district.

On 1 August 1883 the shire's first post office opened in the store of Mrs Honoria Rice at Sylvania but it was many years before residents enjoyed a good water supply. Many relied on home water tanks and the first stage of Woronora Dam was not completed until 1931. In 1917 Cronulla's first electricity was supplied by a private generator, later taken over by council.

A myriad of problems faced early councils, sewerage was still distant even at the conclusion of World War I, and there were demands for piped water, telephones, tarred roads and, in later years, reclamation of the waterways, commercial and industrial development.

Boat Harbour, part of the Holt-Sutherland Estate, was a panorama of sand dunes in 1905. This isolated spot became the refuge for the unemployed during the depression of the 1930s and has, in the post-war years, been subject to extensive sandmining. There are plans for a massive resort development to be located here. (Cronulla Surf Club)

Cronulla Beach Hotel, overlooking North Cronulla Beach, replaced the old Oriental Hotel in the early years of this century. This hotel was demolished in the 1950s to make way for the present North Cronulla Hotel. (Mitchell Library)

The first Cronulla School of Arts, constructed in 1907, was located on the corner of Curranulla Street and Surf Road. These institutions were important community centres and often provided the only local library services that were available. The present School of Arts which houses the Cronulla Theatre was erected in 1913-14. (Descendants of John Hill)

A prominent earlier councillor and president of Sutherland Shire was C O J "Joe" Monro (1883-1966). He was first elected to the council in 1914 and was on 12 occasions president.

He also entered State politics and served in parliament for 12 years as MLA for Georges River and later the electorate of Sutherland. It has been said, as an enthusiast of the shire, he "sold" Cronulla for the benefit of the whole community. He is remembered in Monro Park, Cronulla.

Just prior to World War II a proposal, supported by Monro, was made to form a new municipality covering Cronulla, Bundeena and Kurnell and a portion of the A riding of Sutherland Shire to Gannons Road with a population of 6,000.

The size of Sutherland Shire was emphasised, even without the National Park. It was three times greater than the St George area, then covered by the councils of Bexley, Hurstville, Rockdale and Kogarah. It was considered the Sutherland area would be the industrial heart of the shire while Cronulla remained residential.

Some saw the separation plan as parochial and put forward a series of points to maintain Sutherland Shire as a whole. With the outbreak of World War II, although Monro called for the proposal to be held over, the plan died with a whimper during the war years.

Sutherland Shire's population grew steadily. By 1933 it had reached 13,526, by the end of World War II in 1945, 27,880, by 1986, 175,191. As a new century approaches the population exceeds 200,000 and new challenges are ahead.

Early Days in Cronulla

To the Aborigines the area was Kurranulla, "a place of pink sea shells", but in 1827 Surveyor Robert Dixon (1800-1858) named it the Cronulla Beaches although by 1840 the beach had reverted to Kurranulla. Behind the beach, among the low dunes, particularly at Boat Harbour, were Aboriginal middens. Frank Cridland, writing in 1924, says:

Cronulla Beach is noted for its "pippies" – the bivalve, mostly pink-coloured, from which the seaside resort almost of a certainty takes its name. The habits of pippies are interesting. In size and shape, externally and internally, they are very like an oyster, except that the shell is smooth and even on both sides. They allow a wave to wash them ashore; as it recedes, they turn over on their edges, part their double shells, thrust their tongues (really its foot) into the sand, and in about four separate pulls drag themselves under the surface. Frustrate one in his first efforts to get under cover, and he will probably wait a minute or two before making a second attempt. Their flesh is splendid bait for beach fishing.

The Cronulla area was once part of the Holt-Sutherland Estate, which held a 99 year lease of Thomas Holt's estate. The company encouraged Captain Springall, a retired master mariner, to take up some of the land and he leased five acres at an annual rent of £3 an acre from 6 November 1888 and built a hotel. Springall's Oriental Hotel was a wooden building in an isolated area, his customers mainly sportsmen and Sydney residents who wanted a change of air. The hotel provided Ladies' and Gentlemen's bathrooms; smoking room and observatory, a dark-room for photographers, and bridal parties and picnickers were catered for. The beaches and sea air proved a popular attraction.

In the *Illustrated Sydney News* of 31 October 1889 an article entitled *Our Holiday Resorts: Cronulla Beach* states:

The hotel [the Oriental] is situated in a spot which commands a most expansive view of the coast. The best thing you can do is to climb up into the smoking room, situated at the very summit of the house, which when lit up at night, forms a recognised light for the coasters, which trade between Sydney and Wollongong, and have a look round. In front lies the picnic

Cronulla Park had, by 1930, assumed its modern design. It is fenced off from cars, the horses have disappeared and the trees, although small, are growing nicely. Substantial buildings line the western side of Gerrale Street (on right). (Cronulla Surf Club)

The Cronulla periscope, photographed by M C Hinder, c. 1915. Arthur Rickard, described as the "biggest speculative subdivider" in Sydney at this time, advertised his development of Beach Park Estate (located between Hume, Mitchell, Elouera and Wyanbah Roads) on the side of this building. Rickard visualised real estate opportunities where others saw only uninhabited sandhills. (GPO, Mitchell Library)

ground – a flat clothed in short green herbage, and shaded by dark blue-green mangroves, their leaves grey-tinted where they are up-turned by the wind and catch the reflection from the sky. Beyond this flat are the sand-dunes which fringe the beach, covered in many places with brilliant green creepers; beyond these again are the waves breaking upon the beach. To the south you can see the entrance to the Port Hacking River, the view being bounded by Jibboom Point. It is near to the rocks of the northern headland, where the schnapper most do congregate, so that you can get splendid fishing within a quarter-of-a-mile from the hotel. To the west you look over Goonamatta Bay, sheltered from the strong south-easters, with calm water suited to boating. Here Mr. Springall, the proprietor of the Oriental, keeps several boats for the use of visitors. If you are fond of oysters you should seek this spot when the tide is low, and you can eat your fill. Turn now to the north, and you can see Woolawarre Bay glittering in the sunlight, and beyond, the faint outline of the city of Sydney, enveloped in mist and smoke.

On 27 August 1889 the *Inflexible*, a 128 foot Sydney Harbour steamer, used as a tug, and bound for Sydney, foundered on a submerged object and quickly sank. The crew of six men launched a dinghy and rowed to Port Hacking where a message was sent to the village of Gunnamatta and with help from settlers the sailors were conveyed overland to Springall's hotel. Here they were succoured and returned to Sydney the following day. An inquiry into the

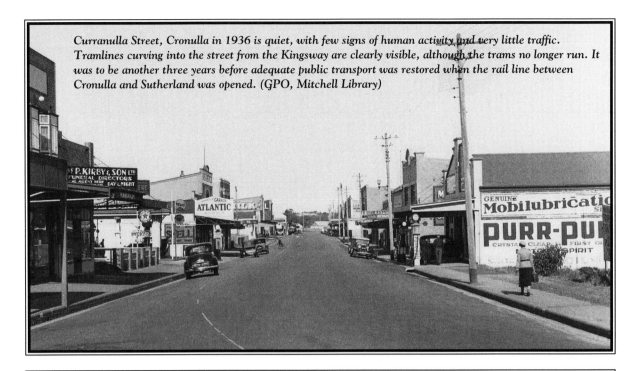

Curranulla Street, Cronulla in 1936 is quiet, with few signs of human activity and very little traffic. Tramlines curving into the street from the Kingsway are clearly visible, although the trams no longer run. It was to be another three years before adequate public transport was restored when the rail line between Cronulla and Sutherland was opened. (GPO, Mitchell Library)

The Kingsway, Cronulla, was a two-lane road with gravel shoulders in 1948. The summit of the hill is dominated by the picture theatre. This building was a landmark from the time of its construction in 1928 until 1997 when the site was redeveloped. Only the facade of the old building now remains. (GPO, Mitchell Library)

A busy day at Cronulla in 1933, although not everyone is dressed in beach attire. The building, on the left constructed in 1926, housed the Cecil Cafe on the ground floor while the second floor was used for banquets, luncheons and dinners. The Cecil Ballroom (top floor) was the scene of fiercely contested dancing competitions held every Saturday night in summer. (GPO, Mitchell Library)

wreck found the sinking of the vessel somewhat mysterious.

Springall held his land and hotel for four years, it was then leased to successive owners. By 1895 the government was subdividing land on the peninsula from Surf Road south and lots were offered for public auction for approximately £10 an acre. There was only the hotel, a few huts and a wharf at the time of the subdivision. Land was set aside for public buildings, including a school and mechanics' institute. Hungry Point was reserved for defence purposes but later became the site of the fish-hatchery. There were further land auctions in 1897 and 1900 and around that

time Albert Giddings and his wife owned a store in Cronulla. By 1906 Giddings was the official mail contractor with the first post office operating in his store. Giddings was a licensee of the Oriental Hotel but renamed it the Cronulla Hotel. Earlier Captain Springall had held a post office agency.

Until 1899 Cronulla still had no official name and had not been proclaimed a township but when the government resubdivided an area bounded by Surf Road, Gerrale Street, Post Office Avenue, Waratah Street and Gunnamatta Bay this section was named and proclaimed the Village of Gunnamatta "in the District of Liverpool" on 25 November 1899. This name was revoked on

26 February 1908 when the whole settlement officially became Cronulla. There were about 200 residences, mostly weekenders. At the time land at South Cronulla sold for £2 to £4 per foot for residential purposes. By 1910 Cronulla was as a small fishing village, a popular but sleepy little holiday resort, with two butcher's shops, several stores and a planned Methodist church. The commencement of the Sutherland – Cronulla tramway in 1911 attracted visitors to Cronulla and the beaches. However, even in 1915, it was still seen by some as a country area and men employed by the department of public works were paid country rates and travelling expenses.

For many years Cronulla retained its village atmosphere. There was no industry although the shell grit from the beaches was sold commercially in the late 1930s to Marine Shell Products on Burraneer Point. There were confectionery and tea rooms, Philpott's stables which offered horses for hire, vegetable gardens, cows and "chooks". A pig farm existed where later the Cronulla High School would rise and a dairy where the golf course was formed, and another dairy at South Cronulla.

By the 1920s Sutherland Shire Council advertised the attractions of Cronulla with a Blanks & Co slide at picture theatres which proclaimed "FILL YOUR LUNGS WITH PURE AIR AT CRONULLA – Surfing, Boating, Fishing, Oysters – ¾ Acre Still Water Enclosed Baths, Continental Bathing".

The *Daily Telegraph News Pictorial* of 15 November 1927 carried the announcement "Hotel Cecil Cronulla – The Best Situated and Appointed Tourist Hotel in Australia – Now Open for Inspection and Business" and the paper

The Surf Queen Competition parade in Gerrale Street on a hot January day in 1927. The procession and crowning of Phyllis Stroud as the "Sun Surf Queen" has been described as "one of Cronulla's greatest processions and most outstanding pageants". This was not simply a beauty contest but had the serious purpose of raising money for St George Hospital which was, like other public hospitals, heavily reliant on community fundraising. (Cronulla Surf Club)

A Broadhurst postcard in 1920 of weekend holiday-makers out in their motors at the beach. Haphazard parking was allowed in Cronulla Park at this time. Horses are, however, in a fenced enclosure on the southern side of the park and tree plantings are protected by tree guards. De Leurence's guest house, the long building with verandah on the right, was popular with visitors. The beach pavilion, topped by a rotunda, is on the left. (Cronulla Surf Club)

carried a full description of the hotel in Gerrale Street. The hotel catered for 150 guests but the dining room could accommodate 180 and offered views over the park and to the ocean. The paper declared the 70 bedrooms were fitted with "carpets of exquisite design" and the colour scheme throughout the interior "is blue and gold, the selections having been made by Mrs Monro, wife of the owner. The building outside is cream and green". The architects of the hotel were Messrs Moore & Dyer of Sydney and the builder Mr C Gray of Hurstville. It was stated:

With unbounded faith in the future of this district, the proprietor, Mr C J Monro, erected a fine building of three stories on the ocean front adjoining the hotel. It comprises a large cafe and oyster bar, a banquet hall capable of seating 600 people, and a magnificent ballroom to accommodate 1000.

The hotel became a popular honeymoon spot during the 1930s. In the 1960s the ballroom, gardens and tennis courts of the Cecil were sold and the site redeveloped. By the late 1980s the Cecil had been demolished, except for the facade, and a 15-storey apartment block and shops built on the site.

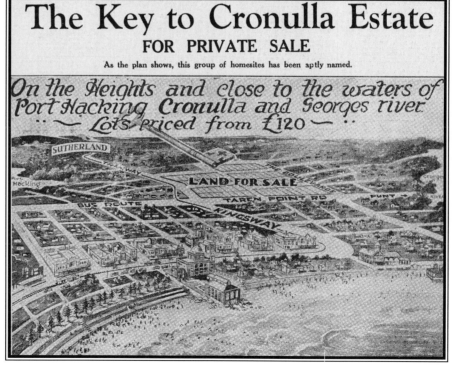

The Key to Cronulla Estate
FOR PRIVATE SALE
As the plan shows, this group of homesites has been aptly named.

On the Heights and close to the waters of Port Hacking Cronulla and Georges river. — Lots priced from £120 —

An advertisement in the Daily Telegraph Sunday Pictorial on 4 December 1912. These high-rise buildings existed only in the imagination of the real estate agent. Despite a flurry of speculative subdivision at this time, Cronulla remained a resort of weatherboard and fibro holiday cottages until the 1960s. Many contemporary real estate advertisements, particularly after the opening of the Sutherland-Cronulla tramway, used proximity to Cronulla as a sales pitch. (Kingsclear Books)

The Lure of the Beaches

Once Sydney's beaches offered balmy sea breezes, sparkling ocean waters and some were surrounded by bushland full of native flowers. The Cronulla beaches – Cronulla, North Cronulla, Elouera and Wanda – stretching along the curve of Bate Bay were a great attraction. In addition the other Cronulla beaches are Shelly Beach and Green Hills, the latter north of Wanda.

Bate Bay was once Whale Bay as great herds of whales passed the coast here as they migrated from the southern seas to the north Pacific seas to breed. The area seems to have been Bate Bay this century but the name was not officially recognised by the Geographical Names Board until 1973.

With the lifting of the daylight ban on swimming in 1906, beaches attracted body-surfers. There were no houses at Elouera and Wanda was considered useless for building. There were risks in surfing and some of the young men attracted to the sport decided it was necessary to found a surf club, one of the first in New South Wales. (Bondi is officially recognised as having formed the first Surf Bathers' Life Saving Club in 1906 although Bronte, from its annual reports, claims to have been as early as 1903). Local swimmers had met informally at the southern end of the beach in 1906 and, in 1907, a meeting was held at the Cronulla School of Arts which resulted in the formation of the Cronulla Surf Life Saving Club. Among those who attended this meeting was Joe Monro, later to become a councillor and president of Sutherland Shire, Lance Giddings (their family store was on the corner of today's Gerrale Street and Laycock Avenue and there was also a depot for the horse coaches which plied from Cronulla to Sutherland Station) and Neville Cayley.

Neville William Cayley (1887-1950), who became a noted ornithological artist, also served as club secretary. Cayley's mother had a boarding house in Cronulla and Cayley was a friend of poet Henry Lawson, who rented a cottage at the Bonnet, on the banks of the Woronora River at Como.

The first clubroom was an old Sydney tramcar located at the beach but Sutherland council

Joyce Carter and Marjorie Congreve on Cronulla Beach in 1930. These modest costumes may have been acceptable in the water but not on the sand and certainly not in the street. There was much fretful anxiety concerning both male and female bathing attire at this time. Cronulla was expected to be "a little better than other beaches" and there were demands that immodest bathers be prosecuted. (GPO, Mitchell Library)

Surf Carnival, Cronulla, 1964. Oars are shipped and crews from as far afield as Coolangatta are ready to compete in boat races. Freddie Lane was a Coolangatta photographer who specialised in photographing surf carnivals. (GPO, Mitchell Library)

Cronulla Beach, c. 1890s. Windswept native vegetation and magnificent sandhills, north of Cronulla Beach, were a feature of what was described as an "out-of-the-way" place. Picnics, horse-riding and fishing, but not body surfing, were popular activities at this time. (Mitchell Library)

A Carlton series postcard of Cronulla Beach, circa 1930. A busy day on Cronulla Beach and, on the right, surfers, with cars, are starting to patronise North Cronulla Beach, despite warnings on the dangers of surfing at this location. (Cronulla Surf Club)

agreed to build a new clubhouse, and casualty room, which was officially opened at the annual surf carnival on Easter Monday, 13 April 1909. In 1913 Cronulla Surf Club acquired another new clubhouse, opened by Varney Parkes, MLA. Cronulla's first surf boat had been acquired from Bronte, a vessel called the *Surf King*, a catamaran style craft of two kapok stuffed torpedo shaped tubes with seating for three paddlers. It finally disintegrated and was buried on the beach.

Early white settlers had noted the Aborigines in the surf at Manly but it was the 1880s before body surfing was introduced. Tommy Tanna, a young gardener living in Manly, who came from the New Hebrides displayed his skill of catching the breakers. He quickly taught a local 17-year-old boy, Freddie Williams, and surfing began to spread along the Sydney beaches. Duke Kahanamoku (1890-1968) from Honolulu, Hawaii, who was a world champion swimmer, was invited to Australia in 1914 by the Australian Swimming Federation to take part in Australian competitions. He was surprised at the lack of surfboard riders on the Sydney beaches. It was already a popular sport in California, USA. While there was a small number of surfboard adherents in Sydney, Duke Kahanamoku's visit popularised the activity and he is usually credited with introducing the skill to Australia. He bought some sugar pine and carved himself a surfboard and demonstrated his dazzling skill at Freshwater Beach. He later gave the board to a 15-year-old Manly youth, Claude West and subsequently it was acquired by Freshwater Surf Club.

Duke Kahanamoku also visited Cronulla in February 1915 before leaving Australia. He and his party were met at Sutherland Station and taken for a tour of the Lady Carrington Drive at

Cronulla kiosk and tearoom, 1930. Sutherland Shire Council spent large sums of money in the 1920s on the construction of facilities at Cronulla Beach. On the right is the third clubhouse constructed for Cronulla Surf Life Saving Club in 1923. This building now houses the Cronulla Sports Complex. (Cronulla Surf Club)

Cronulla Beach, 1964. There was still a mixture of the old and new buildings on the shore line between Cronulla and North Cronulla Beaches at this time. (GPO, Mitchell Library)

National Park. After lunch at Audley the group boarded a ferry to Cronulla, and the beach and surf. Afternoon tea was served in the Park Pavilion before the journey back to Sutherland for a farewell ceremony. At Cronulla, also, Duke Kahanamoku presented a surfboard to a surf club member, Ron "Prawn" Bowman. W G "Bill" Marshall, a former captain, president, life member and noted historian of Cronulla Surf Club, says the board was sold to "Fred Locke, who in turn, signed it over to the inimitable Jack McTigue. Jack, chivalrous character that he was, gave it to a certain beautiful surf siren but alas she married another (ungrateful hussy)."

Another remarkable swimmer from Sutherland Shire, who presently resides in Cronulla is marathon competitor Susie Maroney. On Tuesday 13 May 1997 she completed her amazing swim from Havana, Cuba to Key West, Florida a distance of 179.2 kilometres in just over 24 hours. (Her departure time was 1.46 am Sydney time on Monday and arrival at 2.17 am Tuesday). This was Susie's second attempt at the crossing. The earlier attempt in June 1996, a swim of more than 38 hours, was not recognised. As a sufferer from asthma at a young age, Susie had attended the NSW Asthma Foundation swimming classes at Cronulla and Sutherland.

Visiting Japanese swimmers Katsuo Takaishi and Takashiro Saito pictured with Phyllis Stroud "Sun Surf Queen" in front of the surf club on 26 January 1927. (The Cronulla Story, Mitchell Library)

Cronulla Beach c. 1908. Old tramcars were used as change rooms for bathers and one served as a temporary clubhouse for the Cronulla Surf Life Saving Club until the first clubhouse was erected in 1909. The substantial residences on the "Point" were replaced, from the 1960s, by a clutter of high-rise buildings. (Mitchell Library)

Cronulla is reputed to have one of the best surfs but in 1911 North Cronulla was declared dangerous because of the rips, a particularly treacherous one known as "the Alley" is located at the southern rocky end of North Cronulla.

The North Cronulla Surf Life Saving Club was formed in 1925 and they had a small shed where home units now stand, at the bottom of the Kingsway.

Cronulla Beach, photographed by Charles Kerry c. 1911. A day at the beach was a popular outing for the many Sydneysiders who caught the train to Sutherland and then transferred to the tram running to Cronulla. Cronulla Surf Life Saving Club's first clubhouse, erected in 1909, is on the right. (Cronulla Surf Club)

In that first year the lifesavers of North Cronulla rescued 24 swimmers swept to sea. It was not only surfers that the lifesavers rescued for in 1933 a fishing boat foundered off the bombora at Boat Harbour during a southerly gale and lifesavers bravely rescued the fishermen. On Saturday 15 February 1997 the Surf Life Saving Sydney branch announced that surf lifesavers had rescued 142 people that day from strong rips and collapsed sandbanks and one of the busiest beaches was North Cronulla where 36 rescues were made.

The opening of the Sutherland – Cronulla tramway in 1911 naturally brought people to the weekenders and the beach. It was said that after the introduction of the tram "anyone who compared the place today with only five years ago is astonished at the changes that have taken place".

In 1919 one young couple ran into trouble and the *Hurstville Propeller* of 21 February reported that at the Kogarah Police Court Blanche Shying and Henry Cerchi admitted lying on the beach at Cronulla clad only in bathing costumes.

A Charles Kerry photo, c. 1900, of what is now North Cronulla Beach and Dunningham Park. This area has undergone significant changes. The removal of the frontal dunes, on the left, prior to World War 1 has had a dramatic impact. (Cronulla Surf Club)

99. Cronulla Beach & Park. N.S.W.

Cronulla Beach and Park, c. 1930. A complex of buildings has developed round the beach by this time. The beginning of the Esplanade, one of Sydney's great walks, is visible. Immediately beneath are the Ladies Dressing Rooms. Although these were demolished many years ago the post holes from the old building can still be seen in the rocks. (Cronulla Surf Club)

Each accused was fined ten shillings with costs of six shillings. In November 1934 the *Daily Telegraph* declared "AT LAST – trunks and brassieres for women bathers at Cronulla! The 1935 costumes are being worn on the beach."

So far no action has been taken by beach inspectors. Some of the costumes worn have lattice-work connecting the trunks with the brassiere ... Now that the women have given the lead at Cronulla, trunks for men will probably be introduced."

With the opening of the railway in 1939, Cronulla became the only beach located on a railway line and also with the longest platform in New South Wales, next to Albury. Families arrived with rugs, thermos and picnics to enjoy the main beach, or nearby small sandy beaches, the rock pools or parks. The lifesavers, with their distinctive red and yellow caps, patrolled the beach as crowds wandered from the trains to Cronulla, North Cronulla and to Elouera and Wanda. Since the 1890s the beaches have receded with erosion and conservation programmes have included the planting of marram grass and protective fencing.

Also necessary was "The Wall", a huge concrete armoured construction, built to protect a damaged area of the beach from the sea between North Cronulla and Elouera.

Beyond Wanda lies a low vegetated area of mounds called Green Hills which once led to the famous Cronulla sandhills. The sandhills were used in the epic film *Forty Thousand Horsemen*, obscured the Kurnell refinery from Cronulla and were used for recreational purposes such as hang gliding. Sand extraction diminished their original size. In later years they have been used for the film *Mad Max III* and in television commercials.

In the 1960s families went to Cronulla for their holidays. Chris Henning writing in the *Sydney Morning Herald* (24 January 1994) recalled:

Lots of people came to Cronulla by car, but lots of others arrived by train. Most would

Cronulla Beach 1930. A flat surf but still a busy day at Cronulla. Men's swimming costumes are a mixture of the old style and the modern bare-chested look. (Cronulla Surf Club)

come out of the station and walk straight ahead over past Garling's chemist shop to the beach, or turn left up Cronulla Street to the beach … past the red brick church and the red brick blocks of flats, with white painted windows and pale venetians, you come to Gunnamatta Park and the baths. There, in about 1960, they held learn-to-swim classes.

Sutherland Shire Council supported the lifesaving movement at the beaches and the Surf Lifesaving Club at Cronulla, North Cronulla and both Eloura P C Boys' Surf Life Saving Club and Wanda Surf Life Saving Club which formed after World War II.

The council also recruits professional lifeguards to ensure the safety of the millions who enjoy the beaches each year.

In addition to the beaches a walking track winds around the peninsula and the area boasts six beaches, four ocean baths and the baths at Gunnamatta Bay.

It was on the shores of Gunnamatta Bay that an outdoor amphitheatre was built to stage John Antill's ballet *Corroboree* for the Bicentenary of the Captain Cook's landing in 1970. Antill (1904-1987) was a resident of Cronulla and said he was stimulated by Aboriginal music he heard at La Perouse. The music of *Corroboree* had premiered at Sydney Town Hall in 1946.

By the 1980s the holiday guest houses of earlier years had vanished, to be replaced with high-rise units and in February 1989 the Cronulla Bicentennial Plaza, built at a cost of $7 million, opened to serve a new generation.

Puberty Blues

Cronulla and the beaches hit the news when *Puberty Blues* by Gabrielle Carey and Kathy Lette was published in 1979. The book blurb declared:

At 13 and 14 Kathy Lette and Gabrielle Carey were surfie chicks. At 15 and 16 they ran away from school, turned hippie and hugged trees. At 17 they started singing as the Salami Sisters. At 18 they began writing Puberty Blues *because they realised that youth wasn't all the fun it was supposed to be.*

The two girls from Sylvania caused a storm with their exposé of sex and surf while the newspapers and television stations gave wide coverage to the book which the publishers explained was "about top chicks and surfing spunks – and the kids who don't make it – in a world where only the gang and the surf count".

The two young authors wrote:

The beach was the centre of our world. Rain, snow, hail, a two hour wait at the bus-stop, or being grounded, nothing could keep us from the surf. Us little surfie chicks, chirping our way down on the train. Hundreds of us in little white shirts, short-sleeved jumpers, thongs and straight-legged Levis covering little black bikinis. We flocked to the beach. … There were three main sections of Cronulla Beach – South

Cronulla, North Cronulla and Greenhills. Everyone was trying to make it to Greenhills. That's where the top surfie gang hung out – the prettiest girls from school and the best surfies on the beach. The bad surfboard riders on their 'L' plates, the Italian family groups and the 'uncool' kids from Bankstown (Bankies) swarmed to South Cronulla – Dickheadland.

Recently in the *Sydney Morning Herald* (8 March 1997) Gabrielle Carey wrote:

When Kathy Lette and I published Puberty Blues *we never bothered to consider the repercussions of writing stories based on real people. We just watched the storm of reaction – whose winds still whistle round the streets of Sylvania – as it puffed and puffed and almost blew the entire suburb down.*

Bruce Beresford, with Limelight Productions, produced a film of the book, with Nell Schofield and Jad Capeija in the main roles. The film was said to have a cult following in Cronulla but caused controversy among local inhabitants.

Both the writers survived the *Puberty Blues* frenzy and are still writing, Lette is based in London and Carey in Sydney.

Waxheads outside the North Cronulla Hotel in January 1982 for an article in the Sydney Morning Herald on surf culture and Puberty Blues. This very Anglo-Celtic crowd of "skippies" demonstrates the fact that Sutherland Shire (with 82% of the population born in Australia) has the lowest rate, in Sydney, of people born overseas. (St George and Sutherland Shire Leader)

Highfield – Caringbah and the E G Waterhouse Gardens

The Port Hacking Road, surveyed in 1865, connected the district of Port Hacking with Sydney and followed earlier tracks. It commenced at Sylvania and ended at land held by pioneer Patrick Dolan, approximately half way between Caringbah and Lilli Pilli. There were early tracks branching off through the bush to Horse Rock Point (Sylvania); Highfield (Caringbah) and to Bottle Forest (Heathcote). The latter met the Illawarra Road and closely followed the line of the Princes Highway. Another track roughly followed the later Sutherland – Cronulla Road. The roads were later named by the Holt-Sutherland Company and mostly built by the company when it assumed control of Holt's estate and started to lease land.

The origins of the name Highfield are unknown and in the 1880s the area of today's Caringbah was mostly market gardens. After 1900 much of the old Holt-Sutherland Estate was sold. Although sales were gradual, poultry farms and orchards began to predominate.

In 1918 Woodcock's Farm had 500 peach trees and 2,000 chickens. The first store,

Caringbah, a busy shopping centre, February 1964. This was where McDowells, the first major department store in Sutherland Shire, chose to locate a branch store in 1961. (GPO, Mitchell Library)

Highfield Cash Store, opened in 1904, in Port Hacking Road. It was operated by Joseph Nelson and he built a larger store in 1918 which was inherited by his sons.

Nelson was 84 years when he died in 1927. He had come to the district as a result of the 1890s depression.

In 1911, with the commencement of the Sutherland – Cronulla tramway, the name Caringbah was adopted. It is the Aboriginal name for the small marsupial, the pademelon or red-necked scrub-wallaby, but is said to be a corruption of the actual Aboriginal word. No doubt the arrival of the steam tram caused some excitement for the market gardeners and poultry farmers as it was said that, on occasions, if the tram was heavily laden the passengers had to help push it up the steep Miranda hill. Long after the tramway, Archibald Tickner had a petrol pump in the front yard of his house at Caringbah and later opened the first motor garage in the suburb.

In 1925 a school opened at the corner of Port Hacking and Burraneer Bay Roads with Mr A McGuiness as headmaster although it was the period following World War II when development really began. Shortly before war's end there was a call for a public hospital and a public meeting in Sutherland School of Arts on 9 February 1944 attracted 300 people. In April 1945 the site was chosen on land owned by the Lehane family at the corner of Kareena Road and Kingsway and is now the Sutherland Hospital, Caringbah. In 1948 President Avenue extended only as far as Laguna Street and there was a rough track to Miranda Road. In heavy rain, storm water would cut deep gullies as it plunged down to Yowie Bay. The creek now incorporated into the E G Waterhouse National Camellia Garden had tangles of blackberry along its banks and local children collected them to take home for blackberry pies.

At Caringbah, on the shores of Yowie Bay, is the E G Waterhouse National Camellia Gardens. On 1 November 1968 Sutherland Shire Council convened a meeting of citizens to organise a committee to plan events for the celebration of the Bicentenary of Captain Cook's voyage of 1770. Subsequently the Chairman of the Horticultural Committee, Eric Utick, suggested that Kareena Park, Caringbah be transformed into a camellia garden.

The recommendation was approved by Sutherland Shire Council on 24 March 1969 and the garden opened on 18 July 1970 by Lady Cutler, wife of the Governor of New South Wales. The garden was named in honour of Professor E G Waterhouse, OBE, CMG

Yowie Bay, taken from Yowie Bay Hotel. Frank Cridland, businessman and amateur historian, claimed that Yowie Bay was, before surfing became popular, the holiday capital of Sutherland Shire. He had been a visitor to the Bay in the 1890s and recalled how he had fallen in love with this "deep-water, well-sheltered bay, with good fishing right at hand". (Mitchell Library)

The view from Malvern Road, Miranda, looking towards the city, c. 1900. Miranda, the rural heart of the Sutherland district, was originally known as the "Old Farm". (Mitchell Library)

Official opening of the Parke-Davis Ltd factory on 26 November 1954 with five hundred guests (including local, State and federal politicians) in attendance and Woolooware Bay in the background. The establishment of this factory marked the beginning of light industry in North Caringbah, an area where market gardens and poultry farms had been the norm. Here the formal attire of the dignitaries, accompanied by their wives, is a marked contrast to the laboratory coats and uniforms of the workers standing at the back. (GPO, Mitchell Library)

(1881-1977). Professor Waterhouse was a world authority on camellias (his home Eryldene and its garden at Gordon on Sydney's North Shore is preserved and opened to the public by the Eryldene Trust).

Waterhouse was born at Waverley, Sydney and attended Sydney Grammar School and received his BA degree with first class honours in French, German and English. After a career teaching at Kings School, Parramatta, and Sydney Grammar he studied in Germany. In 1924 Professor Waterhouse was appointed Professor of German at the University of Sydney.

In 1950 Waterhouse, with others, formed the Australian Camellia Research Society with a worldwide membership of approximately 1,500. The Society, with Sutherland Shire Council, is responsible for the garden at Caringbah.

Camellias first appeared in the western world in 1792 when Captain Connor of the East India Company carried the species from China. It is thought the Chinese may have substituted the flowering variety whereas the captain believed he was carrying *Camellia sinensis,* the commercial tea camellia. William Macarthur, son of the famous John Macarthur, may have introduced the first camellias to Australia in 1831 when he sent trees to Camden Park. However, there is a very old camellia at Elizabeth Farm, the Macarthur's original Parramatta property. Botanist Michael Guilfoyle, who operated the Exotic Nursery at Double Bay from 1851, also bred camellias.

At the E G Waterhouse National Camellia Garden camellias and azaleas were planted among the native blueberry ash, tree ferns,

Professor E G Waterhouse inspects the site of the future camellia gardens at Caringbah in 1969. (Mitchell Library)

sassafras, eucalypts and Christmas bush. In addition the gardens feature a collection of silver variegated box elder, elms, tallow wood, pistacia, maples and dawn redwood. The lovely gardens overlook Yowie Bay. In 1827 Surveyor Robert Dixon surveyed and is said to have named Ewey Bay, an Aboriginal derivation of "yowie" or "ewie" meaning "echo". It is also said the name derives from the fact that Thomas Holt employed Scots and Yorkshire shepherds and the female sheep, ewes, were taken to the area to produce their lambs which in the shepherd's dialect was a "yowie". From the 1880s Yowie Bay was popular for fishing and the first lessee on the

bay was Matson, who established pleasure grounds which became a popular attraction.

Weekenders were built along the shores of the bay and the deep waters gave access to boats at all times. Blackwood's was one of the early boatsheds to cater for visitors and boxers trained for their fights in the area. Close to Neales Inlet, Turtle Road, Caringbah, is said to have been named for the many turtles that were once found in Yowie Bay. Residential lots were created from 1910 but Yowie Bay remained a holiday area during the 1920s until the shire's surfing beaches gained prominence. Extensive residential development began in the 1950s.

Yowie Bay Hotel as featured in Country Life magazine in 1911. These two buildings make up what local historian Merle Kavanagh, who lived here as a child in the 1940s, has described as a "hotel, hospital and home". The hotel ceased functioning in 1918 and the following year it served as an emergency hospital during the influenza epidemic. (Mitchell Library)

View from Miranda Public School, c. 1900. Looking down Wandella Road towards the Georges River there are only a few scattered dwellings in this rural scene. (Mitchell Library)

Tram Smash at Miranda

*T*he *South Coast Illustrated Tourist Guide* of, 1924 cost one penny to purchase and included facts on Miranda:

situated between Sutherland and Cronulla; trams to and from Sutherland about every hour, three sections; fare right through, 3d. Times of journey, 15 minutes. Miranda will become an important little township; it is also the centre of the district, and the public school is the central school, to which children from the surrounding districts are brought in coaches subsidised by the Government. There are already three stores; a Post Office, and a butcher's shop at the junction of the main road from Cronulla to Sutherland, with the Port Hacking Road and that leading to Tom Ugly's Point. Lovely views can be obtained in all directions from here. The Post Office is connected by telephone with Sutherland. It is at this point that the visitor to Yowie Bay should alight from the tram, the distance being only a short mile.

It was on a Monday, 10 November that same year of 1924, on a grey overcast day, that the tram consisting of steam motor 88A and three cars departed from Cronulla junction at 6.40 am for Sutherland Railway Station to connect with the 8.30 train bound for Sydney. The tram carried businessmen and a few holiday-makers returning from a weekend visit. The driver of the tram was Samuel Wyche, 54 years of age, who lived in Sutherland and had been working on the tram for just on a month. He, however, had some 30 years experience as both a conductor and driver. The tram also carried the conductor C Thompson.

On a steep slope which descended to Miranda at the foot of a hill the engine left the tramlines and was soon followed by the first wooden carriage down a 15 foot embankment. The second carriage was only partially derailed and, miraculously, the third carriage remained intact on the tramline. It was later reported by the *Daily Telegraph* (11 November 1924) that the tram was:

travelling at between 30 and 40 mph ... a great speed ... in order to successfully negotiate the steep grade approaching the Miranda section, the tram has to come down the incline from Cronulla at a high speed. Residents of Cronulla who frequently use the service have been forecasting disaster at this point for many years. Passengers said the speed was greater than ever before and it is thought the locomotive had gone out of control. The driver had began blowing his whistle shortly after the tram had commenced to gather speed and it was still shrieking when the crash came. Another theory is that a too sudden application of the brakes when travelling at such a high speed caused the engine to jump the metals.

The Cronulla - Sutherland steam tram accident when the tram lost control descending the hill at the Kingsway and crashed over the embankment. (Kingsclear Books)

CRONULLA BEACH TRAM.

Cronulla Beach steam tram, c. 1920. The tram service operated from 1911 to 1931, but was hampered by the use of outdated rolling stock brought from other parts of Sydney. A lack of flexibility in timetabling and the challenge from motor transport eventually made its operation uneconomical.(SPF, Mitchell Library)

World Wars and Depression

At the outbreak of World War I in August 1914 Australia was 12,000 miles away and its citizens intent on the Irish crisis, Davis Cup matches and the approaching federal elections. Australians knew little of countries like Serbia and yet Britain's declaration of war was greeted with excitement and enthusiasm. Australian Prime Minister Cook declared "Remember that when the Empire is at war, so is Australia at war" while the leader of the opposition, Andrew Fisher stated "Australians will stand beside our own to help and defend her to our last man and our last shilling".

The Australian government offered to send 20,000 men to England but such was the enthusiasm that number had been filled before the end of the month and by the end of 1914 enlistments had reached 50,000. The reasons for enlistment were varied. In 1966 a study recorded memories of the soldiers of World War I. "My motives for enlisting were more or less a combination of patriotism, the call of high adventure and a desire to see the world". Another declared "I held the firm conviction that Australia, the fair land of my birth, was in peril of Despotic rule of Germany". Some stated social pressures such as being shunned by "the fair sex" because of a refusal to bear arms. Others felt "adventure was a main reason, going away

The driver, Sam Wyche, of Auburn Street, Sutherland, was crushed underneath the engine and it was felt his death had been instantaneous. The conductor and some 50 passengers had a remarkable escape from death owing to the fact that two carriages remained upright. The passengers' injuries were not of a serious nature. Most suffered from shock and some 13 were taken to hospital. Although it was a scene of chaos local residents arrived to offer help soon after the accident as did Drs Miller, Sanbrook, Sproule and Broome. Matron Spring's private hospital at Sutherland was used as headquarters.

The engine of the tram was totally wrecked

but the only damage to the coaches was the breaking of the glass. Nearly every door and window in the first car was smashed and a considerable number in the second car were also damaged. Later in the day a seven ton crane arrived to clear the wreckage but it proved to be too light and an accident crane from Eveleigh was organised.

The steam tram motor was finally taken to the workshops at Randwick and scrapped. The driver was buried the following day, his cortege left the Wood Coffill Chapel in the city for the Regent Street Mortuary Station to be conveyed to the Rookwood Necropolis.

with your mates was often spoken of". Another said that "at the time I was getting 18/6 for a six-day week and in the army I got 42/- per week for a seven day week continuous time especially in France".

Australia's population was 4,875,000 and by the war's end 417,000 had enlisted for service in the forces. Of these almost 60,000 died and 152,000 were wounded. There were hard years both for the serving forces and the wives and families left behind but peace was celebrated with gusto. In 1919 in Paris a peace conference adopted the principle of a League of Nations. In 1920, in Australia, the Returned Services League was formed.

Two men from Sutherland Shire had served in the Boer War, troopers Laycock and Meeve, and in the years leading to World War I many military exercises were held in Sutherland Shire, particularly in the National Park. Typical of the shire men who enlisted were John and Will Popplewell of Bangor who joined the AIF. Their story is contained in a quarterly bulletin of the Sutherland Shire Historical Society. John was 18 years and six weeks when war was declared and was soon after enlistment sailing overseas. He landed at Gallipoli with the 3rd Battalion. His brother, Will was 21 years, and also served at Gallipoli with the 4th Battalion and was wounded in the knee and found himself in Nemros Hospital in Egypt.

He returned home briefly in 1916 and then went to France and was captured by the Germans. He survived the war, married an English girl and eventually came home to the Sutherland area in 1922.

At war's end Sutherland Shire erected war memorials with stone from the demolished Sutherland House. The Sutherland War Memorial was unveiled on 27 May 1921 and in Cronulla Park a German gun was placed on a concrete slab in 1922. A number of these war trophies were given to various councils. Another memorial stood at Miranda Central School but

was removed following a school fire in 1966 to Seymour-Shaw Park. In earlier years there had been controversy over the figure of a digger on the memorial. In 1919 its removal from the memorial had been called for as it was felt not to represent a typical Australia soldier and was said to be unsightly. When the dismantled monument was re-erected in the park it was minus the

Temporary houses photographed in 1958 by the NSW public solicitor. Cronulla resident, Jim Sherratt, recalls seeing dwellings such as these between Kirrawee and Sutherland stations in the late 1950s as he went past on the train. (GPO, Mitchell Library)

digger, originally sculpted by a Mr. Evans.

The Sylvania sub-branch of the Returned Sailors and Soldiers' Imperial League of Australia (RS & SILA) was formed in 1934 with a membership of ten and met in a hall owned by the Church of England. The TPI (Totally and Permanently Disabled Soldiers' Association) had as co-founder, a Sutherland citizen, Guido F L C Weber. Weber, himself, had been badly wounded at Passchendale in 1917 and had the idea of the organisation while a patient at Randwick Hospital. Guido Weber was Honorary Secretary of the TPI in NSW and Honorary Secretary of the Sylvania sub-branch of the RS & SILA. Daphne Salt writes in some detail of the formation of the organisations in her *Gateway to the South First Stop Sylvania.*

Following World War I there was a world-wide outbreak of pneumonic influenza, or Spanish influenza, which resulted in the death of 20 million people. In Australia 10,000 died. Local councils provided facilities for compulsory inoculation of residents and in Sutherland Shire an emergency hospital was established in the old Ewey (Yowie) Bay Hotel. Among the victims in the Sutherland area was one of the shire's councillors, C E Paine, who died of the virus, and a daughter of the Headmaster of Miranda School, Olga Chiplin.

After the war and the influenza epidemic, Australians again followed the Davis Cup and the cricket. Voting in federal elections became compulsory in Australia in 1925 and in 1926 the famous Russian ballerina, Anna Pavlova, toured Australia and received great adulation. In 1929 there was financial panic in Wall Street, New York, which lead to the depression. Australia suffered severely because the economy relied on oversea's loans and on the sale of primary products. As shops closed, farms were abandoned and debts mounted. Unemployment climbed and for a period more than 30% of the workforce was out of work. It was the era of "jumping the rattler" (travelling free on goods trains in the hope of finding work), of Happy Valley settlements of unemployed, of door-knockers and pedlars desperately trying to sell mothballs, writing pads, soap, pins, rabbits, even bunches of gum leaves. Each State had a system of relief for the unemployed and many found themselves "on the susso" or sustenance, an unemployment benefit. Those who lived through the depression years rarely forgot the experience.

In Sutherland Shire those entitled to relief money had to collect it in Sutherland or at a grocery shop in Sylvania, although here only goods and not money were given for their work tickets. In Cronulla an Unemployed Ladies'

Cronulla Voluntary Aid Detachments (VAD) in King Street, 1917. Voluntary Aid Detachments were made up of women who served as auxiliaries to the Medical Service in World War 1. In peacetime such groups did voluntary hospital work. (GPO, Mitchell Library)

Committee was formed and they sought permission to run a soup kitchen at the school. There were shanty towns at Menai, Sutherland, Bundeena and Kurnell. The desperate collected seagull eggs from Bundeena to supplement their rations but found the birds themselves too salty. A local garage owner claimed that during the depression, those fortunate to still have a car, endeavouring to make the tyres last, cut the beads off the worn tyres and stretched them over the tyres already on the car. Some relied on the fish and shellfish available on the waterways of the shire for food while others recalled that as children it did not make much difference to them "as everyone was poor". Unemployment did not drop to pre-depression levels until 1937.

On the night of 3 September 1939 at 9.15 Prime Minister Robert Menzies spoke to the people of Australia and declared: "It is my melancholy duty to inform you officially that, in consequence of a persistence by Germany in her invasion of Poland, Great Britain has declared war on her and that. as a result, Australia is now also at war".

During World War II about 550,000 men and women, one in 12 of our population of seven million, served outside Australia. Recruitment followed the announcement of war and many men from Sutherland enlisted in the 45th Battalion, St George Regiment. At home in Australia life changed, there was a tremendous war effort, petrol rationing was introduced and rationing of clothing and footwear began in June 1942; tea, butter, sugar and meat rationing in July.

All Sydney's beaches were protected with barbed wire entanglements, cement pyramid tank obstacles and gun emplacements. The Sutherland beaches complied and Cronulla had an anti-tank ditch and a volunteer Defence Corps took up residence in the surf club and dressing areas. Booms of wire netting were erected at Botany Bay and Port Hacking and small vessels impounded to stop enemy infiltration.

There were blackouts and local air raid wardens appointed and some people hoarded food. Public air raid shelters were provided and some families built one in the back yard.

The bridge at Tom Uglys was to be demolished, should there be an invasion, to slow the enemy. Car headlights were dimmed or masked and identifying suburb names vanished from buildings such as post offices. The National Park was again used for training in small arms, mostly by volunteers not able to serve in the forces because of age or health. Following the defeat of the Japanese at the Battle of the Coral Sea, the threat to Australia was no longer imminent but newsreels showed the war in Britain, Europe and the Pacific.

On 7 May 1945 victory in Europe was announced (VE Day). Rationing, however, continued and it was 1947 before it ceased on sugar and meat, clothing in 1948, and butter and tea in 1950. Petrol rationing was finally abolished in February 1950.

Bert Adamson, one of the Botany Bay Tabbigai cliff dwellers, 1969. Although these dwellings were described in 1969 as "landmarks of rugged individualism", the National Parks and Wildlife Service regarded them as "illegal occupations" fit only for demolition. (SPF, Mitchell Library)

Cliff Dwellers of Kurnell

Desperate times find desperate solutions and during the depression a group of men sought shelter on the high sandstone cliffs of Tabbigai Bay near Kurnell. Here on the rocky ledges, with sweeping ocean views, they built a series of shelters, or cliff eyries, wedged into the sandstone.

Tons of rock were dug out to widen and level the natural sandstone ledges and the men trudged two miles across the cliffs and scrubland to bring supplies from the ferry. Suburbia eventually reclaimed the men with the exception of one rugged individualist, Bert Adamson. For over 40 years he remained perched in his cliff side residence, leasing the site from the government for a small amount and paying a few dollars in rates.

He was not entirely without comfort for, with time, he added "mod cons" to his series of walkway connected rooms. His floors were cemented and carpeted and his walls scraped and painted in bright colours. Adamson rigged up a gravity fed, cliff top, charcoal purified, 600 gallon rock tank and fed it into the house by a series of channels so that his bath had running hot water and the kitchen was resplendent with a stainless steel sink. Bert also provided himself with home generated electricity. A post and rail fence ran along the walkways and he had a tunnel to a fishing box where he dropped his lines to the ocean far below. On sunny days from his windows he enjoyed the view of the entrance of Botany Bay and when storms and gales lashed the cliffs, Adamson was secure in his unique home.

Another reminder of the depression years is at Boat Harbour, north of Cronulla, on the Kurnell Peninsula. Some of the shacks built by the unemployed survived to be enjoyed by the more affluent of a later age. The remaining shacks are on private land, once part of Holt's estate.

Botany Bay Tabbigai cliff dwellings, 1969. These ingenious and precarious-looking dwellings were demolished by the National Parks and Wildlife Service in the early 1970s. They received media attention in 1969 when, prior to the Cook bicentenary, Cook's Landing Place was extended and "cleaned up". (SPF, Mitchell Library)

Cronulla Public School

*I*n *Cronulla Public School, The Early Years*, Pauline Curby researched and wrote the origins of the school. Henry Tonkin arrived in Cronulla in January 1910 but it was an inauspicious start to his new life as he had extreme difficulty in renting a cottage because of the summer visitors to the beach. Tonkin complained he was unable to find even a four room cottage for less than 30 shillings a month.

Tonkin became the first principal of the new Cronulla Public School and proved to be an able and innovative man. His pupils long remembered the school excursions which lead them over the local rocks, and to Wattamolla, for the headmaster was interested in geology. He established a junior and reference library to assist children in other studies; conducted a miniature rifle range and initiated life saving classes under Frank Stroud, who was a founder of the Cronulla Surf Club. In fact the senior boys of the school formed a junior surf patrol during World War I. Tonkin was also Secretary of the School of Arts and a life member of Cronulla Surf Life Saving Club.

Cronulla Public School opened in January 1910 and stood on the site of Monro Park. It was a small wooden school with corrugated iron roof consisting of two classrooms, hatroom, lunch cupboard, veranda, lavatory and teacher's room.

It had been a local battle to have a school established by the Cronulla School Association and the later Parents & Citizens Association, headed by a local boat builder, John Hill. At the official opening the minister for public instruction had travelled from Sydney and he and his party were met at Sutherland Station, lunched at Boyle's Hotel, then travelled by coach to Audley and motor boat to Gunnamatta Bay, along the Hacking River which was considered a more pleasant trip than the dusty coach trip from Sutherland.

From 1893 to 1907 there had been an earlier school attended mainly by pupils from three local families – the Laycocks, the Hills and the De Leurences. In fact the school stood on the De Leurence property (now Burraneer Park). The school later moved to the corner of Burraneer Bay Road and Gannons Road where in 1952 the Burraneer Bay Public School was built on the same site. However, there had been a ministerial decision to centralise educational services and, without consultation, the little one teacher school closed in 1907. The children were then to attend Miranda School (established 1893) which involved more travelling. The Laycocks were rowed from Bundeena to join the other children to take Giddings' coach to Miranda. On one occasion a coach overturned and parents were nervous about sending the children so far, especially the younger ones. A school inspector visited and travelled on the coach to investigate the complaints and found the children "seemed to enjoy the ride".

Eventually after some delay, as it was claimed that no site under £300 to £400 per acre could be obtained, the school was constructed. Being

Gerrale Street, c. 1910. Cronulla was becoming more closely settled at this time, although it was still regarded as an "out of the way" place. (Mitchell Library)

close to the camp sites there were complaints of intrusion by the campers who were accused of stealing the school's plants and flowers and trampling the gardens, of camping in the weather sheds and littering with broken bottles and paper. The local cows also wandered into the school grounds. The headmaster also complained of a lack of space at the school and because of a shortage of teachers during World War I, classes sometimes consisted of 55 or 44 pupils, although in winter school numbers decreased because the holiday-makers had departed.

In 1922 a new school site was purchased for £4,000 but it was three years before this school was built close to Gunnamatta Bay. Although the pupils could enjoy swimming lessons at the Gunnamatta Baths there was the problem of the

mud swamps at the head of the bay. Parents complained their children were constantly catching colds and finally land was reclaimed and the mud swamps became Tonkin Oval, named for the first principal.

Many pupils had happy memories of the annual school excursion to Kurnell by Bardsley's buses when they travelled via the Taren Point punt to La Perouse, and then the excitement of the ferry trip to Kurnell. Empire Day on 24 May (Queen Victoria's birthday) was an important occasion and, to celebrate, the children had a half day holiday. It was a patriotic age when children sang *Three Cheers for the Red, White and Blue* and could chant the names of the Kings and Queens of England from William the Conqueror to George V.

The fish hatchery at Hungry Point, South Cronulla, was originally located at Cabbage Tree Creek near Bonnie Vale. It was moved to this site in 1907. This became the location of the CSIRO Division of Fisheries and Oceanography from 1938 until 1985. In that year the New South Wales Department of Agriculture (NSW Fisheries Research Institute) took over the site. (Mitchell Library)

Cronulla Fish Hatcheries

In 1874, 400 acres of the Cronulla Peninsula was set aside for defence purposes. Following the depression of the 1890s all but seven acres of the land was put up for purchase in 1895 at the Crown land sales. This remaining seven acres at Hungry Point was to become the State Fish Hatcheries.

When the village of Cronulla was laid out there were some 40 quarter acre allotments and the rest of the land became small orchards of two or four acres each. The land sold from £7 to £8 per acre.

In 1902 the Hungry Point land was dedicated for use as a fish hatchery and operated from c. 1907 under the supervision of a Norwegian fisheries expert, named Harald Kristian Dannevig (1871-1914). He had been brought to Australia by the fishing authorities. The purpose of the hatchery was to study the biology and ecology of marine life in the hope of establishing a prosperous fishing industry off the Cronulla coast. The

numerous spawning ponds and hatchery were under the control of the keeper, Frank Aldrich. However the hatcheries were closed in 1911 as it was felt there was insufficient commercial interest. The old wharf at the hatchery survived and the area was visited by holiday-makers.

Dannevig was lost with all other hands on the *Endeavour* in December 1914. The ship left Macquarie Island with Dannevig and his staff and was not heard of again. The fish hatchery was later managed by the CSIRO and the site of the former hatcheries is now the NSW Fisheries Research Institute.

Origins of Sutherland

Once the country, now recognised as Sutherland's main suburban area, was covered by a forest of turpentine and ironbark. The turpentine (*Syncarpia glomulifera*) often grows to over 40 metres, with a straight trunk and deep fibrous bark. As a timber it is resistant to fire damage and durable in saltwater. For this reason it was often used in the construction of wharves such as the Finger Wharves at Walsh Bay in Sydney. It was a highly regarded timber and milled extensively for structural purposes such as telegraph poles and beams. To the Aborigines of the Illawarra area it was "Booreeah". Its leafy head made it an ideal tree to give shelter to animals in a paddock.

The grey ironbark (*Eucalyptus paniculata*) is usually found in valleys with clay soils and grows from 20 to 30 metres with a long, straight trunk. Once it was plentiful on the Cumberland Plain around Liverpool where in 1857 pioneer, William Woolls, noted the trees "extended over a surface of several square miles, sometimes rising majestically to the height of 80 or 100 feet without a branch". The Aborigines of the Illawarra named it "Barremma".

Not surprisingly one of the first industries in the Sutherland area was timber getting. Throughout the shire there was blackbutt, grey ironbark, red mahogany and white stringybark.

In the 1860s Cronulla had stands of ironbark, grey and white gum, mahogany and stringybark. Even after the arrival of the Illawarra railway, timber cutting was still a chief occupation. The forest followed the shale-capped ridges along today's President Avenue and Kingsway, the ridges of the Princes Highway, North West Arm Road and Burraneer Bay Road. With post World War II development the suburbs spread along these ridges and the bush survived only in gullies too steep to build on. Even in the early days much of the forest was ringbarked in order to clear the land. At Quibray Bay banksia, bang alley, casuarina and Sydney red gums were cleared in this manner. One of the red gums which stood on the south-western shore of Woolooware Bay was described "as capable of shading over 1,000 sheep under its beautiful curly branches".

Since white settlement it is estimated Australia has lost 50 billion trees. Under the Federal Labor Government's Land Care Scheme, launched in 1989, it was planned to plant a quarter of a billion trees by the year 2000.

First Avenue, Loftus, August 1946. This row of six Housing Commission homes has changed very little since this photo was taken. Construction of homes by the New South Wales Housing Commission after World War II had a significant impact on the housing stock of Sutherland Shire. (GPO, Mitchell Library)

A variety of vehicles meets the train arriving at Sutherland, c. 1900. Most travellers are hastening to depart except for the group of well-dressed children on the right. An advertisement for "Anthony Hordern's New Palace Emporium" is on the left. It was to be 60 years before any large department store located in Sutherland Shire. (Mitchell Library)

The Sutherland post office, (right) a weatherboard building with attached residence, was located on this site in Railway Parade from 1900 to 1957. The Congregational Church next door was originally located on the corner of Oxford and Robertsons Streets. It was moved to this site in 1912, served as a church until 1924 and was demolished in 1951. (Mitchell Library)

It was one of the nation's longest running and best known environmental repair efforts but with the change of government it was stated that in the 1997 budget the annual $4.3 million provided to Greening Australia for the One Billion Trees programme would not be renewed. More than 700 million trees had been planted, sown or regenerated since the programme began. The Australian Conservation Foundation pointed out that many more than that number had been lost through land degradation and clearing during the same period. The federal government's Natural Heritage Trust funded $364 million National Vegetation Initiative aims to revegetate 250,000 hectares each year.

Concerning the dispute over the origins of Sutherland's name M Hutton Neve in *Bygone Days of Sutherland Shire* relates that Major Mitchell had a hobby of studying Scottish history and that in using the Parish of Southerland he adopted an old Norse naming principle. When the Vikings settled Orkney, Shetland, Faroe and the Hebrides, and also the northern tip of the mainland, they named one of the settlements "Sudrland" or "Southland", it being the most southern settlement. Mitchell named Sydney's southern parish "Souther[n]land in the Hundred of Woronora" and the spelling was followed by Governor Bourke and the executive council, although at a later stage an error in the Attorney General's Department altered the spelling to "Sutherland" for the Letters Patent which legally established the counties.

In 1846 Sutherland's population was said to be 23 males and 18 females all of whom could read and write. By 1861 the population of the area was 34 males and 31 females living in eight houses and four tents. The railway brought land speculators and in 1882, before the railway opened, land at Sutherland was being subdivided in the area bounded by The Boulevarde, Acacia Road, Grafton and Elton Streets. The Grand Parade and Oakwood Street were also subdivided in 1886, the year after the arrival of the railway. Land between the new station and Elton Street was cut into 40 allotments, a hotel and post office established, and the village of Sutherland was born.

Prior to the establishment of the postal service on 1 September 1886 the closest facility was at Como or Sylvania. The receiving office was at the railway station and about 15 letters a day were posted. A weatherboard post office was built in 1891. Small farms developed and despite the modern railway, horse drawn vehicles were still very much a part of local life for in 1890 Samuel Dewhurst opened his smithy in Sutherland. The first school opened in 1887 and the first Parents and Citizens' Association met in Boyle's Hall in 1912.

By 1900 there was a small settlement close to the railway station and the Shire of Sutherland was proclaimed in 1906. In those early years fishermen often walked from Sutherland to Pedersen's Gymea Boat Shed to enjoy a day's fishing. There was no street lighting, the streets were only sulky tracks. Residents relied on tank or well water and had no local doctor, the closest doctor was Dr McLeod at Hurstville.

In September, 1906 Sutherland achieved its first doctor when Dr Rooke opened his practice

Railway Hotel, Sutherland, 1911. Ted Boyle took over the Railway Hotel, Sutherland's first, in 1901. It was demolished in 1937 and replaced by a modern building. Boyle, a civic-minded citizen, also owned the National Hall where dances and other social events were regularly held. This building became Sutherland's first picture theatre when it was leased to Marshall's Pictures in 1921. (Australian Country Life, 1911, Mitchell Library)

Railway Parade, Sutherland, c. 1911. The new tramway shares the street with horse drawn vehicles in Railway Parade (now Princes Highway). (SPF, Mitchell Library)

in East Parade. A police service had been established in Sutherland c. 1900, located in a house at the corner of Flora and Eton Streets in the residence of Sergeant Lewis. Constable Clugston lived around the corner in Eton Street. Later a new police station was built in Boyle Street and by 1927 Sutherland boasted eight policemen, two at Cronulla, one at Como and one at Miranda. Sutherland police had a Harley Davidson motor bike and sidecar from that date.

In 1921 the first motor garage was opened, in the building that had been the Sutherland council chambers, by Marshall Russack. In 1925 he moved to the corner of the Princes Highway and Boyle Lane where he repaired motor cycles, cars and trucks.

A kerbside petrol pump, selling Waratah brand petrol, was installed but Russack found the pump distracted him from his repairs and dispensed with it.

By the late 1920s the premises moved more towards President Avenue and Russack, who worked long hours, opened a Chevrolet dealership. In the 1920s there were a number of fires in Sutherland for in 1927 Bardsley's Motor Garage and five buses were destroyed; on 24 March 1928 Delaney's Tile Works, near Kirrawee were burnt; and in 1929 Mrs Whitfield's weatherboard boarding house and Brinsley's Joinery Works suffered similar fates. Brinsley's, now a council owned property, still operates as a business and during Heritage Week, held each year in April, conducts opening mornings at the Joinery Works and Museum with demonstrations of the old machines. Marshall Russack's mother opened Sutherland's first picture theatre on 26

July 1921 in Boyle's Hall. Marshall acted as both projectionist and engineer and, at interval, raced by motorbike to the Miranda School of Arts to change the reels of film.

One of the usherettes at the theatre was Lilly Collins, an aunt of the television, movie critic and lecturer, Bill Collins. In 1928 a new theatre was built in conjunction with Greater Union Theatres and Mrs Russack was appointed manager. The site of the 1928 theatre later became shops but some of the original facade survives.

In 1924 Sutherland was described in *The South Coast Illustrated Tourist Guide* as 16 miles from Sydney and the closest railway station to Cronulla Beach and Port Hacking:

The township of Sutherland is a most central starting-point for all tourist resorts within the Shire, as it is from here that the tram goes to Cronulla, and also from here vehicles of all descriptions can be hired for the conveyance of visitors. The township presents to the stranger the general appearance of prosperity. There is good service of trains to and from Sydney; by some of them the City can be reached in 35 minutes. There are two hotels, one on either side of the station, in which accommodation for visitors may be obtained. The telephone has been extended to Miranda and Cronulla, which is a very great convenience. The offices of the Shire are right opposite the station, and there are two or three pretty little churches in the township, which add very much to the picturesque appearance.

The Sutherland Hospital Caringbah

Residents of Sutherland Shire were originally obliged to travel to St George Hospital and naturally there was agitation for a hospital "of their own", particularly following World War I. One who organised the agitation for a hospital in 1920 was a veteran of the war, Bob South of Caringbah. However, Sutherland had a long time to wait for the hospital and in January 1949, 232 patients were carried to St George and other hospitals by the local ambulance service.

The land chosen for the hospital was at Caringbah on the site where once one of Thomas Holt's overseers, John Lehane, had a lucerne farm. From 1944 some 16 hospital auxiliaries operated over the years and many local citizens unselfishly gave their time and labour. In 1946 a public meeting was held at Sutherland council chambers when it was decided that the proposed hospital would be known as the Sutherland Shire Hospital and a memorial kiosk would be built to serve the hospital. Extra land was to be acquired for the hospital in 1948 as it was considered the original ten acres was inadequate. Various carnivals and functions were held to raise funds. With public unrest it was announced in 1949 that tenders had been called for the building. A tender submitted by F C Powell and Son for the construction of the first section of the hospital was eventually accepted by the Public

The Pictorial News made the opening of the hospital front page news. It was a newspaper which contributed to the community's knowledge of its health care system. (Sutherland Hospital Caringbah)

Works Department. This would provide for essential services and accommodation for 128 beds. The Sutherland Hospital Board considered this quite inadequate and calls were made for a 228 bed hospital. By 1950, 13 acres of land between the hospital site and the railway line were resumed and vested in Sutherland Shire Council and on Saturday 29 April 1950 the first sod for Sutherland Shire District Hospital was turned by A J Williams, who was presented with a miniature spade which was auctioned for funds.

It was 1955 before the foundation stone of the hospital was laid on Saturday, 3 September by the Premier of New South Wales, J J Cahill. The foundation stone for the Nurses' Home was laid on the same occasion but it was 1958 before the Sutherland Shire District Hospital finally opened. Andrew Gray was another who had fought for the hospital and he handed over the chairmanship of the board of directors to E Seymour Shaw when the hospital opened. The first patient was a Mrs Bardwell of Cronulla who was admitted at 9.30 am on 21 April 1958 and the first baby born in the maternity ward was delivered to Mrs Bessini, who had been admitted on 22 April, at 3.20 am. The first matron of the new hospital was Beryl Bonfield who had served with the Australian Forces in the Middle East and she was to serve the hospital for 11 years until her retirement. Matron Bonfield was later to receive the AM (a Member Order of Australia) in recognition of her services. In fact Matron Bonfield was the only matron of the hospital for the new incumbent was given the title of Director of Nursing.

The hospital had several name changes from

An aerial view of Sutherland Hospital Caringbah, c. 1970. (Sutherland Hospital Caringbah)

Sutherland Shire District Hospital to Sutherland District Hospital, Sutherland Hospital and now The Sutherland Hospital Caringbah. Dr Douglas Ash of Loftus was one who believed the new hospital "really belongs to the people of this shire". The doctor could recall when many of the shire babies were delivered at a small private hospital, San Gerard, at Engadine. This was owned and run by Sister Nancy Taafe and the doctor claimed many of her patients considered "it was like going on holidays for ten days to be spoilt and waited on". When the maternity wing opened at the new Sutherland hospital it was managed by Sister Mary Hampson.

Recently Aileen Griffiths who has served many years on the hospital auxiliary, was delighted on locating the original hospital flag safely folded away in a cardboard box. The hospital motto from its inception was "Endeavour to Serve" and the original nurses' badges featured Botany Bay with Cook's *Endeavour* similar to the design of the hospital flag.

Georges River Bridge

Saturday 11 May 1929 was an important day for Sutherland Shire for it was the official opening of the new Georges River Bridge. For years residents had crossed the river by various punt services but by the 1920s an increase in traffic resulted in long queues often waiting for the punt between Tom Uglys and Sylvania. As far back as 1899 there had been calls for the construction of a bridge but it was 1923 before a Georges River Bridge Bill was actually prepared and 7 June 1924 before the foundation stone of the bridge was laid by the State Minister for Works, Mr R T Ball.

Citizens on both sides of the river must have watched with interest as the first timber piles were driven into the river bed and children observed with delight the divers in their cumbersome diving suits and helmets working from Horse Rock Point. The tender for the bridge had been won by an English firm, Armstrong Whitworth to supply the necessary steel work, and Monier State Pipe Works were

Paramedics and emergency rescue squads work in the pre-hospital care system attending accidents and emergencies. Here police and ambulance rescue attend distressed passengers from the Como train smash on 5 February 1985. In January 1982 Paramedic Services began operating from the Caringbah Ambulance Station, (Sutherland Hospital Caringbah)

A long queue of cars and one horse drawn vehicle wait for the Tom Uglys ferry to arrive. Queues were to get much longer before the opening of the Georges River Bridge in 1929. In the summer of 1926-7 there were often delays of five to six hours to cross the river. (SPF, Mitchell Library)

In May, 1929, the Governor of New South Wales, Sir Dudley de Chair snipped the ribbon that opened the Georges River Bridge. The official party drove across the bridge to Sylvania and afternoon tea. Traffic immediately increased and Sutherland Shire attracted more tourists. (Kingsclear Books)

contracted to build the bridge with the initial cost estimated at £109,731. It was hoped the work would be completed within two years but problems developed regarding the design of the original foundations. The final cost amounted to £307,601. A Sydney newspaper in November 1928 reported of the bridge:

This structure is gradually nearing completion, and will in all probability be ready for opening at Easter time next year. The construction has involved a considerable amount of engineering skill, owing to the difficulty of finding a good bottom in places. [It was felt the bridge would bestow] a very great benefit ... upon the whole of the South Coast and even as far as Melbourne itself, for it is on the Prince's Highway that this immense traffic is carried, and the Highway passes over the bridge.

At last on 26 April 1929 traffic crossed the new bridge prior to the official opening. The bridge was opened on a rain swept afternoon by the Governor of New South Wales, Sir Dudley De Chair (1924-1930). There was considerable pride about the new bridge for it was the longest road bridge in Australia (the Sydney Harbour Bridge was not completed until 1932) and the largest project by a local municipal council in Australia. The cost of the bridge was to be liquidated by a toll and then there erupted the "Affair of the Bridge Passes". Sutherland Shire councillors already held a councillor's pass but the council elected to supply a new pass to serve the same purpose as the former but which would give passage on the Georges River Bridge. *Smith's Weekly* on 21 August 1929 carried a headline "SUTHERLAND SHIRE COUNCIL SENSATION Issue of Free Georges River Bridge Passes to Councillors Amounts to Public Scandal" and the paper charged that each councillor was disqualified from the council by accepting the small blue leather pass. Section 30 of the Local Government Act 1919 stated a councillor is disqualified if he accepts or acquires any pecuniary advantage other than permitted by the said Act. Eventually the councillors resigned, the passes were returned and fresh council elections planned.

Dispute raged over the affair and councillors protested they had resigned, not because they were guilty, but because they had taken legal advice. Polling day was on 5 October and all nine councillors were re-elected with "overwhelming majorities".

The bridge, however, proved a great success for on the Eight Hour Holiday in October 1929 10,551 vehicles crossed the new bridge and the toll exacted amounted to £489.17.6. Motor cars paid sixpence on weekdays and one shilling on Sundays and holidays and there was a range of tolls for motor lorries, motor buses, motor cycles, bicycles, horse-driven vehicles and loose stock. Quarterly season tickets were also available. From time to time there were accusations concerning the collection of tolls.

With time the bridge outgrew the needs of modern traffic and in 1984 work commenced on a new bridge designed by the Department of Main Roads. This opened to traffic in October 1987.

Sylvania – A Sylvan Setting

Sylvania was once part of Thomas Holt's estate and he built his Sutherland House behind Sandy (or Holt's) Point between Gwawley Bay and the Georges River, on the eastern side of today's suburb. Sylvania is on the southern shore of the Georges River behind Horse Rock Point, which had been part of John Connell's 180 acres, which he named Castle Connell, with a "quit rent" of three shillings per year. Connell was required to clear 28 acres, make improvements and erect buildings and fences.

He built a stone cottage on Sandy Point later described by Holt's solicitor, Robert Cooper Walker, as:

a neat four roomed Stone built House, within two attics, out kitchen, and workmen's house at the back … There is a good 5 stall slab stable, and a store adjoining it, which is enclosed with a small yard, at the back of this there is a cart and plough shed; also a good Blacksmiths forge.

Sylvania Bowl, opened in 1961, was for many years a popular venue for competitive ten pin bowling as well as casual games. It was demolished in the early 1980s when Southgate Shopping Centre was under construction. A new bowling alley was included in the shopping complex. (GPO, Mitchell Library)

Road works at Horse Rock Point, Sylvania, c. 1920. A road grader is visible and the ferry is coming in. (GPO, Mitchell Library)

Connell kept cows and chickens and was soon transporting fruit from his orchard to the Sydney market. Following Connell's death in 1849, at the age of 90, the property was inherited by John Connell Laycock.

Above Gwawley Bay there was good eucalypt timber, stringybark, bloodwood, mahogany and banksia. When the land was part of the Holt-Sutherland Estate around 1882-1893 there were about a dozen cottages outside the estate and two shops in Sylvania, including Mrs Small's grocery shop. Daphne Salt wrote the history of the area in *Gateway to the South First Stop Sylvania* and includes information on her pioneering ancestors, the Rice family.

In 1883 approximately 20 children attended a school operated by Clara Rice in a veranda room of her family home. The Department of Public Instruction had repeatedly refused a request for a school in Sylvania and it was 1885 before an official one opened in the Toll House. Clara's mother, Honoria Rice, had begun business in 1873 with a general store near the ferry and became the first postal officer in the Sutherland area from 1 August 1883, operating the service from the store at the corner of Belgrave Street and Illawarra Road. Mrs Rice only retired in 1909 when she was 88 years! Salt describes the local Rice home, Weerona, as "a large weatherboard dwelling surrounded by vine-

covered verandas, their Sylvania address then being given as County of Cumberland, Parish of Saint George, Georges River South, Sylvania".

Honoria Rice (nee Prendergast) came from Brazool, near Galway Bay, Ireland and migrated to Australia in 1849 on an assisted passage available to women. She married a master mariner, Captain William Rice, who came from Sherwood Forest and who later captained Australian coastal traders. The couple and their family became pioneers of Sylvania.

A Christian fellowship was formed in the district in 1886 but Congregational services were held in the Organ Room at Sutherland House in 1884, and later The Lodge, near the gates of the property, was made available by Frederick Holt. A small wooden church was built in 1904. The Anglicans had originally met at The Lodge but then held services in private homes until c. 1900. St Marks, Sylvania was the first Anglican church in the shire and the foundation stone was laid on 25 September 1901. Land for the church was acquired for £30 near the ferry landing, later the site of the Tom Uglys Bridge, on the eastern side of Illawarra Road (later the Princes Highway) and a timber Gothic style church built. The little church had oak furnishings and electric light was installed in 1928. It was used until 1963 when a new church was built and the original church became a church hall and was later used for a pre-school. It is the oldest building in Sylvania, as the Toll House was demolished in 1974.

Sylvania has been called the "Gateway to the Shire". James Murphy, manager of the Holt-Sutherland Estate, is credited with having said of the area "it is such a lovely sylvan setting that I could think of no more appropriate name than Sylvania". Earlier in 1863, however, the village had been named Sylvania by Surveyor Parkinson but the district had once been known as Horse Rock Point. The first Torrens Title subdivision in Sutherland Shire occurred in 1882 around Horse Rock Point on land of the Holt-Sutherland Estate when it was offered for housing lots. The Rice family were active in local affairs attending the Sylvania Progress Association meetings. Clara Rice, for example, sought to have the area of Sutherland House, which had been destroyed by fire, declared an historic site and public recreation ground and sought the establishment of public swimming baths at Sylvania. Clara died in 1940 at the age of 81 years.

Sylvania was a rural area with market gardens, orchards and Samways Dairy. The Samways had arrived from Rockdale in 1889 and acquired ten acres and created their home, dairy, garden and orchard out of the bush. Hancock's market garden was on Port Hacking Road and close to the local Gwawley Creek swimming hole. Local small boys were tempted by his fruit. Hancock also had a passion for orchids and eventually the market garden became an orchid nursery. Other early market gardens were owned by the Partridges, George Kidd, between Sylvania Heights and Oyster Bay, the Wilkinsons and the Bloods on the site of Sylvania Heights Public School. The first shire health inspector, William Gillyard Roberts, also had a market garden where he grew good quality peaches and nectarines, and there were various poultry farms and flower nurseries. Sylvania was also noted for its "splendid crops of quinces and Lisbon lemons".

The steam driven vehicular ferry at Tom Uglys Point getting ready to cross to the southern side of the Georges River. A hand-operated ferry was introduced in 1864 but was replaced in 1882 by a steam punt. A number of these operated until 1929 when the Sutherland Shire Council built the Georges River Bridge. (Mitchell Library)

Labourers, possibly part of an unemployment relief scheme, at work on a section of the Princes Highway between Horse Rock Point and Sutherland in 1922. In 1921 this road had been renamed the Princes Highway in honour of the Prince of Wales who had visited Australia in 1920. (GPO, Mitchell Library)

Local children attended the Miranda Central School travelling by the horse-bus, picnicked and swam at Cronulla Beach or the Gwawley Creek swimming hole and watched the ferry crossings on the Georges River. There was even a village blacksmith, Luke Parbury, who opened his forge on the Princes Highway between Ellis and Endeavour Streets in 1910 and operated until his retirement in 1922.

In 1925 the Sandy Point Estate opened and each lot had a water frontage. Despite this the area was still isolated and little development occurred until the 1950s. Local residents enjoyed fresh oysters from leases on the Georges River and the local swimming baths were finally opened on 30 March 1935.

In 1934 Boomerang Hall was built and used for public meetings and functions, including Red Cross dances during World War II, and a local library in the 1950s. In 1973 it was partly used as a local post office. In the 1930s there were small local shops, including Edwards' which sold groceries, fruit and vegetables, produce and newspapers and also served oysters. In the 1940s it was bought by the Stevens, who still operated the shop but not the oyster bar, and who later ran the newsagency. During the 1940s Dalton's fruit stall was located on the main road and was later acquired by the parents of singer, Helen Zerefos, and the store became Paul's fruit shop.

The parents of tennis star, Ken Rosewall, had a grocery business in the shopping area. In addition there was a small cake shop, Kemp's Pharmacy and Sylvania was home to "Bill the Oyster King", Bill Waller. His kiosk was on land leased from Clara Rice and Waller later sold out

A gentleman in a bowler hat, on right, surveys the quiet scene, c.1900, at Sylvania. Sans Souci can be seen in the distance (Mitchell Library)

to Bill Skelsey, who became famous locally for his nightclub, the Colony Club, later the site of the Sylvania Hotel - Motel.

By the early 1980s a new modern Southgate Centre was created and Kangaroo Point Road was declared to be Sylvania's richest street. Michael Poulson and Peter Spearritt in *Sydney, A Social and Political Atlas* (1981) claimed Sylvania kept pace with the explosion in university graduates from 1971-1976 and had an average income of $22,000, below-average unemployment and higher than average home ownership. Kangaroo

Point on the south-western side of Tom Uglys Bridge is now a suburb and regarded by some as the "Hunters Hill of Sylvania".

Sylvania Heights is on the heights above Kangaroo Point and overlooks Oyster Bay. In 1919 water frontage lots were created along the foreshores.

It too had scattered development until the 1950s when young families began building homes in the area, much of which was still under green-belt restrictions. It was then an area of natural bushland, water views, native birds and animals and, in spring, prolific wildflowers.

An aerial view of Sylvania Waters in 1970, a model of the canal estate, offering most houses waterfront access. (Sutherland Shire Council)

Sylvania Waters

At Gwawley Bay Thomas Holt planned and excavated a series of canals where he had acquired, in 1866 for a fee of £90, from the Crown, a freehold of approximately 180 acres of the waters of the bay. It was never part of the Holt-Sutherland Estate and passed from the Holt family in 1918. The canals were constructed in the marshy foreshores at the head of bay and were to be used in Holt's oyster cultivation venture. The canals, all in neat rows, were about 20 feet wide and four feet deep, with about ten feet between each canal. There were several miles of the canals and all emptied into the main channels. Frank Cridland in his *The Story of Port Hacking,*

Cronulla and Sutherland Shire predicts "Some day, perhaps, a water suburb will be laid out there with waterways instead of macadamized roads. Such an area of freehold tidal waters offers all sorts of novel town-planning possibilities and problems."

In the 1920s the bay was owned by an oyster farming family, the Smiths, but sold in the late 1950s and a syndicate, headed by a former builder and developer James Goyan, acquired ownership in 1960. Sylvania Gardens Pty Ltd proposed to create a garden suburb from 286 acres of Gwawley Bay. The final plan for the marine suburb was to allow for 667 home sites and to achieve this a five mile retaining wall was constructed around the waterfront. The wall was circular and so designed as to allow the water to continue circulating with the tides to prevent rubbish accumulating. The waterways, at the lowest tide, had a minimum depth of two feet.

The new suburb was to have waterways, recreation areas, living, school and industrial sites, roads and shops. The waterways within the estate were to have access to the Georges River and Botany Bay and were to be at least 132 feet wide.

The concept was unique in Sydney and the first stage of the area was offered for sale in 1963 and continued to develop over a ten year period. Both a recession and economic pressures resulted in not all the houses in Sylvania Waters having direct waterfront access. Three islands were created: Murray, completed 1964; Barcoo, completed 1967; and James Cook Island, in the 1970s. On the latter island many of the houses were Mediterranean style mansions with manicured gardens and immaculate waterways. Many of the houses had a cruiser moored at their jetty.

By the 1980s, 50-square houses were selling for around $350,000 and it was stated that:

Sylvania Waters and its islands are all linked to main traffic thoroughfares by a series of bridges. Interestingly, because of link-ups with freeways such as Southern Cross Drive and General Holmes Drive, the trip to the city by car is only about 20 minutes.

On 28 January 1997 the *Sydney Morning Herald* reported that the State government would "rip up" a draft law limiting the construction of canal estates and rewrite the regulations to ban all such developments after strong lobbying by conservationists. Since the opening of Sylvania Waters about 30 canal estates have been built along the coast, from Nowra in the south to Tweed Heads in the north.

Gymea – The Suburb Named for a Lily

A feature of the area south of Sydney are the giant Gymea lilies (*Doryanthes excelsa*), up to three metres in height, with a distinctive pink to red flower head with green leaves at the base. These leaves were used by the Aborigines to weave baskets, as well as strips of cabbage tree palm (*Livistona australis*). The suburb of Gymea was named by the government surveyor, W A B Greaves, in 1855 because of the prevalence of the plant. Gymea extends from between Kirrawee and Miranda to Point Hacking between North West Arm and Gymea Bay.

One of the early landowners was S W Gray, who held 60 acres overlooking Port Hacking and remembered in Grays Point. In 1856 there were Crown land sales from Burraneer Bay including Miranda, Caringbah, Gymea Bay and Sutherland. When the Illawarra railway was planned there was a proposal that it cross the Georges River at Taren Point and on to Waterfall by a route skirting the heads of Yowie and Gymea Bays. Instead, because of property interests at Hurstville, the railway followed its present course to Como.

In 1897 George Smith acquired five acres of land and operated a dairy, the first in the shire, on land now the site of Gymea Technical College. After milking, the cows were released onto Malvern Road (now Kingsway) and would wander down to drink at the creek. George Brewster bought the dairy c. 1914 and his cows used to wander along North West Arm, their cow bells sounding through the bush.

Gymea Bay was a tranquil place with only a boat shed and, from the 1920s, a few holiday cottages. It could be accessed from the water or, alternatively, by alighting from the tram at Miranda and strolling down "a long red road" (Kiora Road). (Mitchell Library)

A horse bus once operated from Gymea Bay to Sutherland and was owned and driven by a man named Warman. He was also the proprietor of boat sheds on Gymea Bay. Among the early families resident in Gymea around 1915 were the Clarkes, Freemans, Morans, Shorters, Hornes, Derreys and Hazes.

The Hornes had a boatshed at North West Arm and life was simple with amusements such as bushwalks and swimming. The first residential subdivision was at Gymea Bay in 1917 but they were isolated waterside dwellings with virtually no transport until a railway station opened in 1939. North West Arm was a tangle of ferns, wildflowers and, of course, the Gymea lilies. In the early 1900s there was still good timber at North West Arm which locals felled and hauled from the gullies with bullocks. On the river banks was pure white sand. A pioneer of North West Arm was a New Zealander, Bob Dashwood, credited with building the first house c. 1911. He later married and the family water supply was the creek, now north of the Grays Point turnoff. Returning with a load of timber in his cart Dashwood was often bogged in Saville's Creek and would walk back to President Avenue to get some assistance from neighbours. People travelled around the district in horse and sulky and it was a rural community with cows, fowls, orchards and vegetables.

The track which followed Coonong Creek down to Gymea Baths was edged with trees, ferns and wildflowers in spring. Earlier it was called Stapleton's Creek for the local landholder who ran the abattoir and established the butchery at Sutherland. In recent times a devoted band

Cramptons Service was located at the corner of Kingsway and Milburn Road, Gymea. It was operated by Thomas William Crampton from 1944. He was a founding member of the Gymea Bowling Club and he sold part of his own property, alongside the service station, to the bowling club for £6,000 in 1958. (Steven Crampton)

of locals, instigated by Ruth Graddon, have carried out bush regeneration covering an area of five hectares.

They won an award for their work and renamed the creek Coonong, an Aboriginal name meaning "running water". The group also discovered evidence of what could have been an abattoir yard in Darryl Place.

In earlier times fishermen would walk from Sutherland Station to Pedersen's boatshed at Gymea Bay to fish in the fresh waters. The area did not develop until post World War II and once local Christmas bells and waratahs were sold for threepence or sixpence a bunch near St Paul's church at Gymea.

There were market gardens, Marien's, around the area of Manchester Road, the Kingsway, Sylvania Road and almost to The Boulevarde. Twice a week the produce of the gardens was loaded onto a dray and carried to the city markets.

Horses and drays were a familiar sight along the Kingsway, portion of which was lined with large pine trees and on the corner of Wandella Road (now Miranda) was a corrugated iron church set among ironbark trees, perhaps survivors of the old forests. The church was the birthplace of the Miranda Co-Op founded by Ted Thacker, Elijah Philips, Mr. Russell, the Fletchers and others. Gymea was advertised as:

Koalas were to be found in the area between Gymea Bay and Sylvania Roads and when the fruit ripened on the many fruit trees in the district the sky was thick with flying foxes.

G A Jones, a fruit inspector for the area of Sutherland Shire, reported in 1911:

I have inspected nearly every orchard in the Sutherland district, and I am pleased to say that the best of stone fruit can be grown in any part of it. I have seen the famous Briggs May peach grown to perfection at Miranda with heavy crops of fruit on the trees. This peach is the best of all early peaches for the Sydney markets.

The post World War II period brought many changes and in the 1950s new streets formed and skeleton house frames appeared in what had been bush.

With new families taking up residence it was rumoured that in one year alone 1,000 babies were born in the suburb. Gymea expanded as a suburb and new businesses opened – a grocer, fruit shop, cake shop, chemist and a doctor and dentist. Schools followed with Gymea Bay and Gymea North Public Schools, Gymea High School and Gymea Technical College for tertiary students.

Abattoirs in Gymea

William Stapleton, a farmer, arrived in Australia with his wife, Mary Anne (nee Thimbleby) and children in 1853 to establish his family in a new land with hope of a better future.

One of his sons, Charles Harvey Stapleton, became the first butcher in Sutherland. His family arrived in the district c. 1880 and built a house in the area of today's Stapleton Street. Here his wife, Elizabeth, grew apples and grapes.

Stapleton's supplied meat to the railway workers on the Illawarra railway between 1884-1886 and also to soldiers training in the area of what is now the Royal National Park.

Stapleton's also had their own extensive slaughter yards around President Avenue to Manchester Road, to Wyalla Road including Sylvania Road, Pines Road and Walker Avenue to Forest Road. Originally the land had been leased from the Holt-Sutherland Estate in 1881. Stapleton's delivered meat six days a week to Gymea and other areas but the roads were rough in the pre-war period.

Aaron Walker, who owned an orchard and vineyard, purchased the slaughter yards. In 1977 a local resident Mick Derrey recorded his

This butcher shop was owned by Thomas "Banjo" Alan Patterson. It was located at the corner of Kingsway and Kiora Road, Miranda. He owned it from c. 1917 to the early 1950s. He also owned abattoirs in Gymea. His land went from Bunarba Road south to the creek, through to Darryl Place. He only owned land on the north side of the creek. (Steven Crampton)

memories of the slaughter yards for Sutherland Shire Historical Society. He recalled the wooden bridge over Dent's Creek and the procession of bellowing bullocks, drovers, dogs and children as the beasts were driven to the slaughter yards. The children would hide under the bridge but the bullocks would refuse to cross until the children were driven out from their hiding place. There were still remnants of the forest to the rear of today's Gymea shopping area on the eastern side of Gymea Bay Road and at the location of Gymea Railway Station the bullocks were yarded. The road descended to the nearby creek and there was a culvert of rough timber and blackberry bushes on either side of the creek. In the yard of the abattoir approximately 10 bullocks and 20 sheep were kept before being taken to the abattoir. Near the orchard and slaughter yard were rough humpies where the bachelor employees of the yard lived. Aaron Walker also had a boiling down works and the tallow was carried in a heavy spring cart to Sutherland Railway goods siding. Derrey also remembered Walker's first slaughter yard at President Avenue and Sylvania Road and the second between Pines Parade and Sylvania Road.

Walker's had a butcher's shop at Miranda and Cronulla. Aaron Walker was the grandfather of the Reverend Alan Walker, the prominent Methodist minister. Later Walker sold the slaughter yard to Patterson who moved the site further along Sylvania Road past Bunarba Road. Derrey remembered Patterson as a slight man who drove his bullocks alone from Sutherland on horseback. Patterson later bought Walker's shop in Miranda.

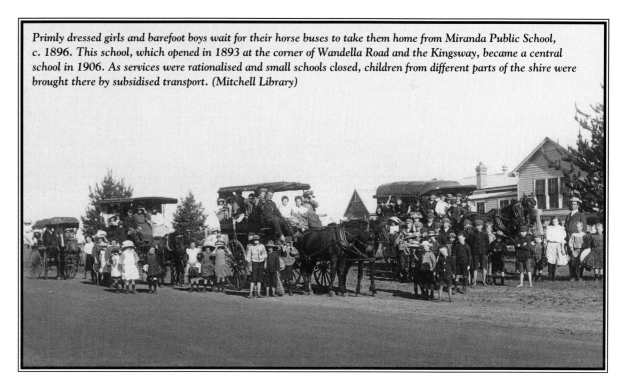

Primly dressed girls and barefoot boys wait for their horse buses to take them home from Miranda Public School, c. 1896. This school, which opened in 1893 at the corner of Wandella Road and the Kingsway, became a central school in 1906. As services were rationalised and small schools closed, children from different parts of the shire were brought there by subsidised transport. (Mitchell Library)

Miranda – Euphonious and Musical

Miranda was originally a portion of John Connell's land and later purchased by Thomas Holt and became part of the Holt-Sutherland Estate. It was named by Holt's manager, James Murphy because he considered it an "euphonious, musical and appropriate name for a beautiful place". It has been claimed to have been named for the Shakespearian character in *The Tempest* and for an estate in Spain. In the 1880s it was also called "Old Farm".

Coming from Sydney, access to Miranda was by way of the Tom Uglys Punt and through Sylvania by a rough track which ran to Sutherland. A horse bus service operated to Miranda from Sutherland and in the 1890s the fare was one shilling. In 1906 the local school was declared Miranda Central School and children from outlying districts attended, some travelling by the local horse bus, but also by private horse drawn vehicles and by foot. The school was burnt down in 1966 Approaches were made to the first Sutherland Shire Council for a passable main road. In 1909 the Miranda Progress Association (founded in

1905), which had agitated for a separate shire rather than be incorporated in the Bulli area, urged council to consider building a bridge in place of the punt. The local farmers had to take their produce via the punt to market. The Cronulla - Sutherland steam tram operated from 1911 and by the 1920s there was a tram every hour and a small residential development.

Miranda was believed to have the best soil in the area and was a rural area with piggeries between Port Hacking Road and Willarong Road South, fruit orchards and poultry farms. Gwawley Creek was fed from run off from Miranda and in heavy rain swirling torrents rushed down to the creek which ran to Gwawley Bay.

In the early 1900s there was Nolan's Miranda Store which was later destroyed by fire. The first post office, run by Mrs Hall, was in the rear of Piper's Produce Store at the corner of Kiora Road and the Kingsway. The present post office stands on a site that was once Walker's butcher shop. Gone are the days when the local butcher delivered by horse and cart with a chopping board and a set of scales on the tailboard.

There were various door to door travellers including Len Fletcher of Miranda who travelled over the shire selling smallgoods in all types of weather. In 1909 there was a hotel at Yowie Bay licensed to the proprietor, a man named

Piper and Penprase Stores, Miranda and Cronulla. Piper's Store at Miranda was rebuilt for Penprases in 1956. The firm had some years earlier also opened a store at Cronulla.
(Pacific Portal, Mitchell Library)

Serbert. Miranda had a police station close to the Congregational church and c. 1918 the local sergeant was a man named Placket, remembered as "a very hard man". Initially his transport was a horse but he later had a motor bike. Following World War I the district attracted soldier settlers who also operated poultry farms and orchards.

In 1911 *Australian Country Life* wrote of the district, "there are several snug little poultry farms". One was owned by a man who originally had been a printer in Sydney and knew nothing about poultry breeding when he arrived:

[He] studied the subject and went to work on business lines, and now my returns from poultry enable me to live comfortably, and I have the healthiest life you can imagine. There is always a demand for poultry, and I can send a crate down to Sydney in the morning and have it delivered anywhere the same day. Although called a tramway [Sutherland - Cronulla steam tram] the service is practically a railway, as freight cars bring our goods from the station at regular hours during the day.

By 1923 Miranda had four shops and the post office and Frank Cridland recommends various walks in the shire and states:

Another easier and short walk may be had by taking the train to Willarong Road (Wine Bar) [Wine Bar was a wooden building in Willarong Road near the Kingsway which gave refreshment to people going to catch the Georges River punt or who had been fishing at Lilli Pilli] and then following that road till it finishes at a precipice at the end of Willarong Point.

From the tramline at Miranda a long red road may be seen dipping down to the gully to the south. Then, rising on the hill beyond, it appears to be swallowed in the distance by the bordering green trees. This is Kiora Road, an enticing walking or driving track that leads to the big promontory lying between Yowie and Gymea Bays. From it by-roads branch to all the little headlands and inlets of the two bays and the promontory.

The original Nelson homestead and store, a simple weatherboard building with two front windows and a door, was still standing in 1950, a larger store had been built in 1904. In the 1950s Samways Dairy from Sylvania still supplied milk by horse drawn cart although motor trucks were introduced later. By the 1960s Samways Dairy had closed and bottled milk was collected from the milk depot and delivered by truck until 1968 when Albert Samways relinquished his milk run. In the 1950s an ex-soldier, George Willock, owned six shops and three flats in Miranda, all occupied by ex-servicemen. He negotiated for the Miranda RSL sub-division to obtain 24 house sites for ex-servicemen and this is now Willock Avenue. Again it was the post World War II era which changed the rural atmosphere and sparse settlement.

In 1964 Miranda Fair opened where once there had been market gardens and a brickpit. The site was purchased by Westfield-Miranda and the original complex was expanded and completed in 1992 making Miranda Fair the largest shopping complex in the Southern Hemisphere.

The Miranda Co-operative Society

In 1886 Edward "Ted" Thacker, often referred to as the "Grand Old Man of Miranda", was the first to avail himself of the opportunity to take up land that had once been part of the Holt-Sutherland Estate. Others soon followed his example, including F W McFarlane (who was to become shire clerk), and established poultry farms, or grew flowers and vegetables.

The Miranda Progress Association was formed in 1904. Ted Thacker, who was active in local affairs, formed the Miranda Agricultural Bureau with others from the Progress Association. This later became the Miranda Co-operative Society and in 1916 premises were built at the corner of Kingsway and Johnston Street. The shareholders of the co-operative were mostly poultry farmers, dairymen and market gardeners. In fact Elijah Phillips, of the Ventura Poultry Farm, was another founding member of the society. The aim of the Co-operative Society was to buy and sell at the lowest possible prices.

The society survived until the 1970s. In 1973 a decision was made to redevelop their Kingsway premises with a new $1 million shopping complex, with motel, restaurant and theatre. The development meant the death-knell of the old society as it went into receivership in 1975 and ceased trading. Miranda was no longer a rural area and had become a suburb for young families. With the development of Miranda Fair in 1964 it became a major retail area for Sutherland Shire.

A general store, Cole & Sons, opened c. 1902 and was the hub of Miranda It was later acquired by Pipers, and claimed to function on "Integrity and Service" under J W MacFarlane, then A C Lowe, who subsequently moved to Scone, NSW. In 1923 brothers Charles and Walter Penprase bought the store and opened as Penprase Bros. It developed a hardware and builders' supplies business and in 1948 the two brothers sold the firm to a company which traded as Penprase (Miranda) Pty Ltd. This store, and a modern Cronulla store completed in, 1948 were operated by Messrs. K G O'Neill, S Inglis, D Inglis and R M Hoskins. The Cronulla store traded as Penprase (Cronulla) Pty Ltd, The Golden Rule Stores, for Builders' Materials, General Hardware and Service.

Miranda Agricultural Bureau Ltd Produce Store, 1921. This store, built in 1916, was part of a co-operative movement that developed out of the Miranda Progress Association. It aimed to give local farmers stronger bargaining power. Miranda, with its fertile farming land, was the most productive area of the shire. (GPO, Mitchell Library)

Miranda Fair Shopping Centre, March 1964. Felt hats were still worn and HMV black and white televisions were on sale when Miranda Fair was opened. This shopping mall, taken over by Westfields in 1971, has become one of the largest in Sydney. (GPO, Mitchell Library)

The Woronora River – Como, Jannali, Kareela, Kirrawee and Bonnet Bay

Located on the land mass between the Georges River and Port Hacking, and bounded on the west by the Woronora River, are the suburbs of Como, Jannali, Kareela, Kirrawee and Bonnet Bay. Before the area was named Como by James Murphy there was only natural bushland, indented with Scylla and Carina Bays on the Georges River, and Bonnet Bay on the Woronora River.

A large grassy area with an abundance of native grasses, kangaroos and a shepherd's hut became known as Double Bay Paddock. The crossing of the Georges River at Como by the Illawarra railway in 1885 gave access to Sutherland and the southern area. The new Como Railway Bridge opened in 1972. The railway meant the progress of Como and it was the terminus point on the south side of the Georges River. Originally just a shanty town for the railway workers, it became a popular area for fishing, boating and picnicking. Crown lands were released in 1887, just a few years after the arrival of the railway.

In the early 1900s George Rollings and his wife arrived in Como and settled at Coronation Bay, then known as Frog Hollow. The Rollings were involved with the establishment of a local Progress Association and members had to be enthusiastic as to attend meetings it was necessary to walk with a hurricane lamp from Oyster Bay or Bonnet Point, or travel by boat along the river. By 1910 land was being auctioned and the area was described as having "pretty sand beaches, sheltered bays, bold headlands and low level water frontages". In 1924 Woronora Park on the river was said to have:

for a long time been a favourite spot for young men to camp out, week-ends and holidays. It can be reached either by boat from Como, or, a short walk from Sutherland through picturesque scenery, with gullies growing all descriptions of magnificent ferns. In the Park the Council have erected shelters and ample seating accommodation. The view from the hill, looking either down the river towards Como or up, is one of the most beautiful to be obtained in any part of Australia.

Woronora is an Aboriginal name meaning "black rock" and the mouth of the Woronora River had been noted by Bass and Flinders during their exploration of the Georges River in 1795. On 14 August 1861 Mort & Co, of Sydney, advertised a farm of 50 acres on the left bank of the "Warronora River" noting there was a track to Liverpool. Norman Price is regarded as Woronora's first settler but he acquired the Swaynes' property in 1899 and they moved down river towards Como. In 1907 a new road from Sutherland, with five zig-zags, was constructed from Sutherland to the Woronora River. At the top of the hill, with fine views of the river, the Swaynes operated a refreshment room. The river, "Wonnie" to the locals, was a Mecca for campers, weekenders and holiday fishermen. Excursions were made to the Cathedral Rock and The Pulpit. By 1936 the river was being dredged for sand between Cathedral Rock and Jackeroo Point by Cement Mortars Ltd. The Land Board, however, laid down conditions for the dredging of the sand.

Weekenders built in the bush introduced some to the pleasures of Sutherland Shire. During the depression others became permanent residents, surviving in rough shanties. Also following World War II the construction of homes by the NSW Housing Commission attracted young couples to the Sutherland area. Development and construction of new roads, such as Bates Drive, allowed new suburbs to develop.

Jannali is another Aboriginal name meaning "moon" or "beautiful moonrise" and the area developed after the opening of the railway on 7 February 1931. Back in 1901 land was subdivided by the Intercolonial Investment and Land Company. One of the early residents were the Tierney family who came to Jannali in 1921. Initially their home was a bag humpy made of corn bags over a timber frame and whitewashed with a roof of iron bark and tin. The only water supply was the local creek and the washing was done in the creek until a well was sunk. Later the family built a weatherboard house and Mrs Tierney was a foundation member of the Jannali Progress Association.

A local, Mick Derrey, recalled being one of a gang unloading the concrete slabs for the station and working after midnight by the light of carbide lights. The men quenched their thirst from a water pipe in the western bank of the railway cutting which was used by the fettlers on the stretch between Como and Sutherland. The area between Box Road, Buller and Robertson Streets, and the railway, was still sparsely populated in 1937. There was one shop facing the railway station and four houses in the bush. The same year, 1937, 24 lots were offered for sale with a £5 deposit per lot and the balance in 12 quarterly payments at an interest rate of returned servicemen and many took advantage of the inexpensive building blocks, erecting homes on the heights of Jannali between 1953 and 1955. However, the ex-servicemen provided road access and Sutherland Shire Council assisted with surfacing materials. Many of the families remained in the area and on 17 February 1979 they celebrated in Rossford Avenue with a street birthday party to commemorate their 25 years in Jannali.

The suburb of Kareela was named in 1968 and the Aboriginal name is said to derive from "kari-kari" which means fast, probably for the area's strong south winds. Alternatively the name is also said to mean "place of trees and water". Originally the area was called Salisbury and residential subdivision only began in 1962. The suburb followed an overall plan and by the mid 1970s the development was said to be substantially complete. The Kareela Golf and

The new road to the Woronora River, 1903. The cottage is there and this is, in the 1990s, still the main road between Sutherland and Menai. Although there was no bridge over the river until 1912, this road made access to the river more convenient for the many Sutherland residents who enjoyed visiting it. The thousands of motorists who travel the route daily observe more vegetation than is seen in the foreground of this photograph. (Mitchell Library)

Social Club, which is on Bates Drive, opened in c. 1977 and the course is 18 holes.

The suburb is on the shores of Oyster Bay and to the north-west are the two relatively new suburbs of Oyster Bay and Caravan Head on the Georges River. Oyster Bay was named for the abundance of oysters grown in the bay.

The land, once part of Thomas Holt's estate, was subdivided in 1901 and an area east of Carina Road, known as the "By the Water Estate", was subdivided in 1912 into residential lots. Nevertheless the area remained relatively undeveloped with unmade roads until the late 1940s.

Early settlers of the area now known as Kirrawee were the Blade family and it was once

Dredging and land development along Woronora River, 1971. The creation of Prince Edward Park Estate and similar developments has transformed Woronora from a placid backwater to a suburb. (Mitchell Library)

Kirrawee, which is Aboriginal meaning "lengthy", was adopted with the opening of the railway station, formerly the suburb had been part of Sutherland.

The old quarry at Kirrawee has walls composed of shale eight to ten metres thick, illustrating the thickness of the local shale, and shale capping extends along the Princes Highway to Loftus. Shale vegetation has an abundance of turpentine, grey ironbark, white stringybark and forest red gum. Sutherland's pioneer and entrepreneur is remembered in the Thomas Holt Village, founded in the 1950s, in Acacia Road, Kirrawee.

Bonnet Bay takes its name from a natural feature, a headland which overlooks the Woronora River is said to resemble an old-fashioned woman's poke bonnet. Located north-west of Jannali and on the shores of the Woronora River until the 1960s the area was unspoiled bushland. It was declared by the Department of Lands in 1969.

The area was known to the poet and writer Henry Lawson who, in the last years of his life, spent considerable time at a hut at the Bonnet, which was a well-known fishing spot. Lawson, who died in 1922, was said to have written in the area.

The Jannali Reserve is off River Road at Bonnet Bay. Spectacular bluffs rise on each side of the Woronora River and within the reserve are two walking tracks, one of 60 minute duration and the other 40 minutes. A sandy beach and sheltered bay were created at the head of one of the backwaters and visitors may canoe on the Woronora River.

called Bladesville. George Blade, his wife and family had a weatherboard house off the Princes Highway on the eastern side of the Sutherland Brick Works. Blade worked on the railway while his wife operated a small mixed goods store and postal receiving office in her home. The family later moved to Urunga.

On the bank of the creek east of the railway station were a number of families living in bag covered houses. The Dube's property ran from Flora Street to President Avenue and their neighbour, Gough's, had land to Bath Road. Both families had flower market gardens and they relied on the creek for their water supply.

Fernleigh

On 30 October 1987 Ivey Alcott died at Sutherland Hospital. Mrs Alcott (formerly Alcock), who was born in Narromine, was well-known in the Sutherland area. She and her husband, Errol Alcott, engineer, boat builder and marina owner of Burraneer Bay, purchased Fernleigh in 1947.

Fernleigh, a National Trust listed property, has been claimed to have been built from as early as 1821 to as late as 1875. Land here was offered for sale in 1856 and the Crown land sales records reveal John Connell Laycock had the title from 9 May 1859 and is said to have financed the construction of the house. From machine made nails used in the construction the house has been dated as c. 1860. Fernleigh was built from local sandstone and roofed with slate imported from Scotland. Laycock mortgaged 40 acres of his land to John Thomas Neale but his own estate was later acquired by Thomas Holt. Holt sold the former Laycock property to Charles York and he named the house, York House and used it as a country retreat. York died in 1880 and left the property to his wife. The symmetrical Georgian house has sandstone walls 450 mm thick and it is believed the mortar used in its construction came from the shells of Burraneer Bay. In the 1860s the surrounding ridges of the property still retained cedar and the joinery throughout the house is Australian cedar. The house overlooks the waters of Burraneer Bay.

At Fernleigh Mrs Alcott maintained a large collection of animals and was said to have the only licensed private zoo in New South Wales. The collection included her pet great Danes and chihuahuas, kangaroos, wallabies, rabbits, an ape, fox, cockatoos, fish, rats, bats named Count Yorga and Dracula who dined on arrowroot biscuits, a monkey named Candy who was partial to cream sherry from a gilded wine glass and her two famous Shetland ponies.

Frank Cridland states Burraneer Point was a favourite haunt of the local Aborigines and the waters of the bay suited their bark vessels. There were rock carvings in the area, one of a whale, another with a shark with a bream inside. W D Campbell, author of *Aboriginal Carvings of Port Jackson and Broken Bay, Memoirs of the Geological Survey of New South Wales*, (1899), photographed some of these carvings. Cridland quotes an A Meston who claimed to have seen the local people encircling animals and driving them through the bush into an inner ring where they were killed with spear and boomerang.

Crown land sales began at Burraneer Bay in 1856 and among the buyers were John Connell, junior, of Kurnell, his nephew John Connell Laycock, Andrew and Mary Webster. The Websters land was sold on several occasions and in 1865 Dominick Dolan bought a block at the head of the bay. His small cottage survives but is now unrecognisable. Dolan died in 1888 and the land was subdivided.

Mrs Alcott maintained a large collection of animals at Fernleigh including her two Shetland ponies. (Neil R. Keen)

Max Hinder photograph of power boating on Port Hacking, c. 1920. Although power boating had become popular by this time, very little special gear was used. The people pictured are dressed in fashionable street clothes for their outing. (GPO, Mitchell Library)

Gunnamatta Bay

Gunnamatta is Aboriginal and means "a place of beach and sandhills" and was once used as the name for Cronulla. Surveyor Dixon marked the bay on his survey of 1827 and the bay is located between the headlands of Cronulla and Burraneer. Once Botany fishermen left their boats at the site of a canal dug by John Connell at the head of Woolooware Bay and cast their nets in Port Hacking, then landed the fish at Gunnamatta Bay and in hand carts wheeled the catch to their boats.

Burraneer Point was once isolated with, Frank Cridland says, an occasional shell gathering launch dropping stone ballast near Yellow Rock, which was later broken up for building purposes. In the early 1900s water frontage land became available under the Holt-Sutherland Estate "free selection" terms. In 1904 Cridland himself acquired a five acre weekend block from the company and stated all blocks ran from Woolooware Road to the water. A surveyor measured the land and it was necessary to

Max Hinder photograph, 1922. Sunbathing had become very popular by the 1920s. (GPO, Mitchell Library)

acquire at least two acres. No fees were charged for the survey and there were no other fees. The land was leased and an annual ground rent paid of £2, £2.10s., or £3 per acre according to the relative value fixed by the company. The lease could be converted to freehold on a 4% basis. The Holt-Sutherland leases gave 99 years' tenure from 1899 but the option to freehold ceased at the end of 56 years, 1 July 1955. Cridland reveals that for at least five years he was considered "a fanatic for taking up land at such an outlandish place as Gunnamatta Bay". Even in 1924 few of the original leaseholders still held their land. Around 1910 Burraneer Point became popular as a weekend resort and Gunnamatta Bay was described as:

For the lady bather and children, the wide stretches of clear, shallow water offer absolute immunity from both sharks and undertow; while the overhanging caves and foliaged knolls along its margin are more than ordinarily picturesque.

By 1937 Gunnamatta Bay was described as a honeymoon paradise.

A number of the early residents of Cronulla, Messrs Atkinson, Windsor and Wilshire called for land at Gunnamatta Bay to be preserved as park area and Gunnamatta Park was proclaimed on 6 September 1895. Here hundreds of picnickers arrived from the inner city areas to enjoy the park sloping towards the beach and baths, or to enjoy the boating facilities. A wharf was built south of the baths and the inaugural trip of the ferry from Cronulla to Audley operated from the new wharf from 18 December 1909. In 1924 *The South Coast Illustrated Tourists Guide* states "The launch excursion between Gunnamatta Bay [Cronulla] and Audley [National Park] is superb, and presents ever-changing views of a veritable fairyland of waters and foliage". The guide describes Gunnamatta Bay as "an arm of the Port Hacking River near its entrance, with its pretty residences nestling

John Hill's boat shed was located at the head of Gunnamatta Bay. Hill was a member of the first Sutherland Shire Council and the inaugural president of Cronulla Public School Parents' and Citizens Association. (Descendants of John Hill)

amongst trees … just inside Gunnamatta Bay the government fish hatcheries are situated". In 1926, during a period of drought, Sutherland Shire Council utilised the creek at the northern end of the park as an emergency water supply for local residents. The creek was fed by a natural spring but the creek was later piped.

Mrs Laycock, a widow, operated a boatshed on Gunnamatta Bay and often fished at the end of her pontoon, or from a boat or canoe. She used a bottle to catch octopus, set lobster pots and gathered fresh oysters off the rocks. John Hill, a councillor on the first shire council and a boatbuilder on the shores of the bay, constructed various types of crafts, including yachts, many of the ferries that plied between Kurnell and La Perouse, and some which operated on the Hacking River, and speed boats. He was said to have the first outboard motor on Port Hacking. Hill had an oyster lease and also grew vegetables. As well as speed boats on the bay, at one period small aircraft at low tide landed for joy flights over the local areas.

A Cronulla sportsman, Jack R Hallett, introduced aquaplaning from the United States of America and demonstrated daredevil stunts on various beaches and bays within the shire. Hallett was a life member of the Cronulla Surf Life Saving Club and a foundation member of the Port Hacking Branch of the Royal Motor Yacht Club.

In 1895, land with Gunnamatta Bay frontages was sold and John Lehane was one purchaser of two acres for £57. Another block of two acres was still available at the next sale in 1897 for £42. Seven acres were reserved at Hungry Point for defence purposes but revoked in 1902 and later became the Cronulla Fish Hatcheries. North of the Fish Hatcheries 11½ acres of the foreshore was preserved as Darook Park.

In 1924 Frank Cridland wrote that the existence of Darook Park:

is unknown to the majority of permanent Cronulla residents. Hidden away in a protected gully running down from Nicholson Parade to Gunnamatta Bay, it is a perfect gem of a park, left in its natural state, except for a winding track cut through the undergrowth to the picturesque sand-dunes and grassy banks of the water-front. The vegetation, owing to the sheltered position and rich damp soil, is dense and semi-tropical, and a complete contrast to that of the surrounding country. The native grape, wild jasmine, and Wonga vine grow there. Creepers and parasitic vines batten on the gum trees.

Cridland adds a footnote that since he wrote the above the park was "improved" by the removal of undergrowth and a fierce fire ravaged the gully. He felt it doubtful that the park would ever recover and regain its former beauty.

At the time there was also an Aboriginal waterhole and large midden in the park and carvings in a cave at the foot of Bay Road (now Bay Lane) which Cridland called for to be preserved. Nearby on a property were other features of Aboriginal art cut into a sloping rock overlooking the bay.

Adjoining the park Cridland notes the white Wahgunyah Cliffs and cave:

The head of Gunnamatta Bay c. 1905 at high tide. These mud flats were drained in the 1940s and Tonkin Oval, now a popular sporting venue, was formed on the reclaimed land. (Cronulla Surf Club)

which used to be such a picturesque landmark from the bay. The ground has been built on lately, and the beautiful formations are being cut away for building purposes. A striking natural pillar of fretted white sandstone which appeared to support the overhanging rock has suffered this fate during the last twelve months.

In the 1940s the Railways Union always held their annual picnic at Gunnamatta Bay, an event which attracted many railway workers and their families. It was a day of rest and enjoyment with children's races and free ice creams and sweets. Work and club picnics are still enjoyed in Gunnamatta Park today. Darook Park offers swimming facilities and a walking track.

Woronora Cemetery – "Where Beauty Softens Grief"

Woronora Cemetery was gazetted and dedicated as a general cemetery, open to all religious denominations, on 2 April 1895. A former mayor of Rockdale, John Bowmer, was instrumental in agitating for land south of Georges River to be set aside for a cemetery. Portion of the land had earlier been used by the Sutherland brick works, which commenced operations c. 1886 and bricks from the yard were used in the construction of Lobbs Hall (c. 1890) in Sutherland. The brick works, which produced sandstock bricks with hand-powered presses fired in an open kiln, met opposition from larger concerns and soon went out of business. Charles Fripp became the first superintendent of the cemetery. Fripp died in 1907 and was succeeded by Tom Smith, who had married Fripp's daughter, Eva. Smith retired in 1952. The cemetery was for internments for the Sutherland and St George districts.

The first interment was conducted the day previous to the cemetery's dedication when Helen Willows, only 19 years, of Kogarah was buried. There was another burial on the 3 April but the first entry in the Register of Burials is Muriel King, 6 months, on 13 April 1895. It has been noted that in the period 1895-1905 41% of the burials were children ten years old or younger. Infant mortality in Sydney at this time was 4,690 as babies succumbed to typhoid, diarrhoea, diptheria, croup and infant convulsions.

As for Rookwood Necropolis, the Regent Street Mortuary Station was used as a departure point for a Woronora mortuary train which began operations in 1885. Drivers were instructed there was to be no speeding and no whistling. Coffins could also be collected at intermediate stations where they were to be placed on trestles at the end of the station platform and passed initially into the passenger luggage vans. At both Sydenham and Kogarah Stations small mortuary sheds were constructed to hold the coffins pending the arrival of the train. An extension line from Sutherland to Woronora Cemetery, covering 38½ chains, opened on 13 July 1900.

There was a single platform 440 feet long and a turning loop for the engine. On arrival at Woronora the coffins were loaded onto a four wheel cart and pulled to the grave. The mortuary train allowed 53 minutes for the service at the cemetery and a bell was rung for visitors to hasten back to the train which departed at 4 pm. The last train to carry a hearse car ceased operations shortly before World War II but it has also been claimed the last service ran on Sunday 20 August 1944. The cemetery branch line closed on 23 May 1947, the platform was demolished and the rail line lifted. District motor funeral services then operated and the Woronora Station was demolished, the bricks being incorporated in the construction of the first United Services Club at Sutherland.

The construction of a crematorium was considered from 1910 but the building, designed in an art deco style "in the modern manner" by architect Louis L Robertson, was not opened until 21 April 1934. At the time cremation was still a contentious issue and this was alluded to in speeches at the opening when some speakers saw it as "a step in the right direction; or a mark of progress and dignified respect". The crematorium originally had a pool of remembrance with fountain and fish but in 1944 over 30 fish were stolen by two young culprits and it proved difficult to maintain the pool. The pool was later covered over and the roof filled in.

Various gardens, including a crematorium garden, were established at Woronora plus two named for writers Mary Gilmore and Henry Lawson. Both the latter gardens feature native trees and shrubs with the Henry Lawson Gardens having rockeries connected by walkways while the Mary Gilmore Gardens feature small gardens on open lawn, surrounded by established trees. The cemetery gardens also contain approximately 12,000 roses.

Cemeteries are of importance historically in providing biographical information and, also, as a means of explaining or demonstrating past practices. Nineteenth century general cemeteries were usually laid out with parallel avenues and separate denominational areas. Headstones of the 19th century are also of interest with stylistic characteristics and Victorian motifs of architectural style. Particularly popular was the Gothic style. Cemeteries also illustrate craft skills in stone, iron and timber. During the 19th century in New South Wales some 350 monumental masons were working. Following the opening of the Woronora Cemetery five monumental masons were working in Sutherland – A Allen, Apex, F Arnold, J Ellis and Scotts. In 1924 Ellis advertised his location as "East Parade Right at Station Sutherland" and offered "Headstones, etc., Repainted Inscriptions Neatly Executed in Freestone, Marble and Granite. Charges Strictly Moderate. Good Workmanship Guaranteed. Country Orders receive Prompt Attention."

A number of notable people are buried at Woronora including William G Judd, the first president of Sutherland Shire; pioneers John Lehane, a native of County Cork, Ireland, who died at Miranda in 1905 at the age of 65 years;

Edward Thacker also of Miranda; William Burns, Senior, the founder of Burns' Timber Yard of Caringbah; and Thomas Holt's eldest son, Frederick, who on 7 February 1902 was struck by a train while crossing the railway line between Katoomba and Wentworth Falls and later died. Frederick Holt was deaf as a result of scarlet fever suffered in childhood and he was unable to hear the approaching train.

Also buried here are Owen Jones of Bangor and Rice family members, early settlers of Sylvania. After the closing of the Devonshire Street Cemetery in Sydney some of the graves were transferred to Woronora.

During the depression some of the local unemployed endeavoured to sell flowers from the bush and gardens in Flora Street near Sutherland

Railway Station to visitors to the cemetery. The number of sellers increased to such a degree, with each endeavouring to be as close as possible to the station, that the police were asked to intervene. The flower sellers were then licensed by the council with bays allocated in Flora Street for their baskets and 14 sellers were allocated spots. However complaints were still received and the council cancelled all licenses from 24 August 1934 and sales were then to be made only from private property.

Michael Boyd has written *Woronora Cemetery and Crematorium Sutherland 1895-1995* (published by the cemetery in 1995) recording the origins and history of the cemetery. In 1995 Woronora Cemetery achieved its centenary and adopted the motto "Where beauty softens grief".

Gravediggers at Woronora Cemetery in the 1940s. Work included putting out bushfires, digging graves with the help of two horses and a dray in the 1930s, sometimes maintaining tools in the blacksmith's shop and sometimes maintaining the gardens. (Board of Woronora Cemetery)

Woronora Dam

Although Captain John Hunter explored to the mouth of the Woronora River in 1789 it was not named until 1827 by Assistant Surveyor Robert Dixon. He chose the name "Wooloonara" said to mean "place of no sharks". Later it became Woronora, Aboriginal for "black rock".

Until the Woronora Dam was built, many residents of Sutherland Shire had to rely on tank water and often suffered severe water shortages. On occasions tank wagons were operated to supply water to residents. The construction of the dam, as well as ending the water shortage, also gave employment locally and one, Gordon Jowett, remembered using about 100 horses from Waterfall for snigging timber and pulling drays on the construction of the road to the dam. He also carried explosives to the dam site. Sand from the Woronora River was used in the construction of the dam. There was a large wooden hopper at "The Island", later Jannali Reserve, and the sand was pumped into the hopper from a dredge by means of a floating pipeline supported by empty 44 gallon drums. In the hopper fresh water was circulated through the sand but some salt remained. Trucks were reversed underneath to load the sand and as the vehicles drove up the hill to Sutherland the water leaked from the truck so the roadway was constantly wet. During the night, sand was carried from the Cronulla sandhills for the construction and obtained from Woronora by day.

The purpose of the dam was to supply water to Sutherland Shire and the areas immediately north of the Georges River. During the period 1904-1910 there was a severe drought but in 1906 the president of the Water Board had collected survey information with the idea of adding part of the Woronora and Georges River catchments to the area supplying Sydney water. It was not until 1925 that a decision was made to construct a dam on the Woronora River and by November 1926 work commenced on the access road and preliminary work at the dam site. It was decided the dam would initially have a height of 60 feet with storage to supply Sutherland and Cronulla and at a later stage increased to 120 feet for general metropolitan purposes. By the end of 1928 a recommendation was made for the building of a dam with a height of 200 feet and a

Woronora Dam wall, 1941, nearing completion. Woronora Dam, constructed between 1927 and 1941, has an operating capacity of 71,800 megalitres. (Sydney Water Archives)

The residents of Sutherland Shire were dependent on tank water until the construction of the Woronora Dam. In times of drought water had to be bought from a tank wagon which did the rounds of residential areas. People at Cronulla were particularly affected in holiday time when an influx of visitors placed a severe strain on their tank supplies. (Kingsclear Books)

capacity of 15,000 mg and a safe draft of 20 mgd, together with the construction of a 42 inch pipeline to Penshurst Reservoir. However by 1929 all operations, other than the preliminary works, were closed down owing to the depression.

In August 1930 the Sutherland-Cronulla water supply scheme was gazetted as unemployment relief work during the depression. The government provided a grant of £71,500 and a loan for the same amount for the dam to be constructed in two stages. Funds were available for the main wall to be built to a height of 45 feet, with storage of 206 mg and to be completed in March 1931. Operations then ceased due to lack of funds. Construction recommenced in November 1935 and concreting

of the major structure commenced in April 1937. The Woronora Dam was completed to full supply level in October 1941 at a cost of £2,100,000. Nearly 1,000 acres of the river valley was submerged when the reservoir was full.

Initially the pipeline was to convey water from the dam to Penshurst Reservoir and ultimately to extend it to Waterloo. Owing to World War II there was a lack of steel available and the pipeline was not commissioned until November 1942. With the expansion of Sutherland Shire the function of the pipeline was to supply Sutherland and Cronulla, Engadine, Heathcote, Helensburgh, Stanwell Park and areas just north of Georges River. The

pipeline, 16 miles long and four feet in diameter linked Penshurst Reservoir and fed the network of mains and was capable of delivering 32 million gallons of water per day. The cost of the pipeline was approximately £930,000.

On completion the capacity of Woronora dam was 15,792 million gallons, with the height of the wall 217 feet and length of the crest 1,350 feet. An arched gravity, blue metal concrete and Cyclopean sandstone structure, the dam was one of the smaller ones in the Sydney system. A zig-zag overflow weir was constructed thus providing a more effective length and an electric lift penetrated the main section of the dam for access to two internal inspection galleries.

The quantity of concrete used was 424,000 cubic yards and the quantity of excavation 151,000 cubic yards. At the crest of the wall the thickness of the concrete was 20 feet and the maximum thickness at the base 185 feet. The safe draft was 12 million gallons per day. The greatest depth of water was 201.25 feet and the full supply level 553, 25 feet above mean sea level. The mean annual rainfall in the catchment area was 42 inches. The dam now stores water from a 85 square kilometre catchment of the Woronora River.

Woronora Dam, together with Manly Dam, are independent of the main metropolitan system. During World War II this meant that in the event of an enemy attack on the main Sydney water supply both Woronora and Manly Dams could have supplied water to Sydney. Woronora Dam is accessible from the Old Princes Highway and opens to visitors and there are barbeque and picnic facilities.

Woronora Township, 1939. These temporary workers' dwellings were erected during the construction of the Woronora Dam. (Sydney Water Archives)

The Woronora Dam Township

The building of the Woronora Dam attracted workers to the area, especially as it was a time of depression, although work was suspended between 1927 and 1941.

In *The Sweat of their Brows, 100 Years of the Sydney Water Board, 1888-1988* Margo Beasley records memories of some of those who lived at the Woronora township. One, Ronald Horni, could not recall how the family arrived at Woronora but felt it was his father's search for work during the depression years. His father had been a seaman and a rigger and later worked constructing silos where he gained a familiarity with concrete construction. He believed this enabled him to obtain a job at Woronora where his son thought he was a foreman. Horni recalled the houses:

They were not large, just little bungalows basically, but they were quite comfortable. They were mostly made of fibrolite and built up on brick or concrete piers because the ground was quite sloping. The fibrolite was not so crash hot aesthetically but it was fairly functional. It was water-proof and windproof, and I suppose that was all that mattered. All the fireplaces consisted of those great big pressed metal hoods attached to an outside wall and the fire was built inside that.

Most of the families were poor but with work at the dam some started to get "a sort of financial independence". Horni recalled his parents having a radio receiver which created considerable interest. They also had a gramophone and a collection of records and entertained friends. Naturally the local children were warned to stay away from the dam construction site as it was extremely dangerous. When blasting occurred there was "a very piercing whistle" which was heard all over the town and then the blast occurred some seconds later followed by a great shower of rocks thrown into the air. "The kids loved that – they lived for it." Horni's father went to work in the country when work on the dam ceased, while the family remained at Woronora, but later they all moved to Western Australia.

Another, William Brennan, recalled the workmen:

like monkeys up on the wall. One part would be over a hundred feet from top to bottom. They had a rope tied around their waist and they had to hang onto a jack-hammer and hoses, and they had steel tied to their backs. You've never seen anything like it.

Brennan recalled some of the overseers who were "legendary in the Water Board for abuses of their power". The work was hard:

You would have the steel on your back and you'd pull them out as you wanted them, put them in your jack-hammer and bore the hole, and then you'd put the shorter one back in the

pouch on your back. When you knocked off in the night, you would have all this gear with you and you would have to pull yourself back up the rope to get up to the job.

The Woronora Dam also had some of its construction work filmed for scenes in the early film, *Dad Rudd, MP*, made in 1939. Bert Bailey, suitably bewhiskered, starred in a series of Cinesound films, by Ken Hall, from the 1930s based on Steele Rudd's characters *Dad and Dave*. A flying fox conveyor was built for the film scenes and many of the Woronora workers and their families worked as extras in the film.

Loftus – Gateway to National Park

Lord Augustus William Frederick Spencer Loftus was Governor of New South Wales from 4 August 1879 to 9 November 1885. He was born at Clifton, near Bristol, England on 4 October 1817. He was the fourth son of the Second Marquess of Ely, privately educated and trained by his father for the diplomatic service. His career in diplomacy was said to be exceptionally brilliant. He served as ambassador in Berlin during the Austro-Prussian and Franco-German wars and at St Petersburg 1871-1879. He then requested easier work in a warmer climate and duly arrived in Sydney as governor.

These Japanese naval officers were among the 30,000 visitors who came to Loftus to view military manoeuvres associated with the Easter Encampment, held annually between 1886 and 1890 at the northern end of the National Park. This area had been cleared of the "wild scrub" that had previously grown in the area. (Sydney Illustrated News, 15 May 1886, Mitchell Library)

His arrival coincided with the dedication of the National Park in 1879 and Loftus in the Sutherland Shire is named in his honour as is Loftus Street in Sydney.

With the opening of the new Illawarra railway the next station to the south of Sutherland, Loftus Junction, was opened on 9 March 1886. In 1896 the name Loftus was adopted. It is bounded to the east by Royal National Park and to the north by Woronora Cemetery and Prince Edward Park and to the west Loftus Creek flows to the Woronora River.

Loftus was closely associated with the National Park and at one time Loftus was used as the name for the whole area of the park. Early development took place on the eastern side of the railway line and by 1893, 2,000 acres had been cleared and planted with grass and some exotic ornamental trees. A shady carriage drive was constructed to run to Sutherland.

Visitors to the National Park arrived by train to Loftus Junction and a horse drawn coach operated via Lady Rawson Drive, over Temptation Creek to Audley Road. The fare was sixpence per person each way.

The area became popular with the New South Wales military authorities, they built Farnell Avenue, and Flagstaff Hill was used for signalling with the heliograph. The signals were sighted by defensive positions in Sydney. Easter camps were held from 1886 until 1914 and the first camp in 1886 attracted 30,000 visitors who were entertained by a military display as they picnicked at Loftus. It was said on the Easter Monday so many visitors arrived it was necessary for the railway to utilise cattle trucks to cope with the crowds.

Subdivision for building lots began from 1923 but development was slow. Local children walked or rode horses to school at Sutherland or some jumped on the passing horse bus on its way to the depot near National Park. Some attended the school over the railway line, through the bush to a school on the waterfront at National Park. Around 1910 a road was built beside the railway line to Sutherland and bakers' carts delivered twice a week to Loftus. Most of the early residents were railway workers or had poultry farms or orchards. Gilhams managed the fibro plaster works near Tenth Avenue and they held cracker nights and the local children watched with excitement as the bright fireworks exploded in the night. In the 1940s the roads were still untarred dirt roads, the railway workers had tents beside the railway line and the old steam trains puffed up the hill.

The Loftus Progress Association was formed after Sutherland Shire Council proposed establishing a sanitary dump for disposal of night soil at Loftus and the Association had its first success in preventing the dump. After World War II the semi-rural land was subdivided into building blocks offered for sale from £50 to £200 per block. Owner-builders constructed their new timber homes in the bush but there was always the danger of bush fires. It was, even in the 1950s, almost a pioneer society for there were no shops, schools, sewerage, water or electricity and only restricted mail deliveries.

Close to the railway line at Loftus is the Sydney Tramway Museum ([02] 9542 3646). The museum is operated by volunteers and visitors enjoy rides on the restored electric trams that once operated in Sydney until their demise in 1961. There are also services at specific times to Royal National Park.

Engadine and Yarrawarrah

Unlikely as it may seem, Engadine was named for an area in Switzerland.

Although much of the surrounding area became part of the National Park in 1879, around 1890 Charles McAlister purchased a large portion of land. McAlister had engaged in pearl fishing off Thursday Island in the Torres Straits. He built a house, which he named Sunbeam Cottage, and established gardens. Later he added two wings to the cottage and renamed the residence Homelea on portion 113 on Woronora Road. Woronora Road was part of Mitchell's original Illawarra Road. Following an overseas trip and a visit to the Engadine district of Switzerland, McAlister and his wife noted the hills and valleys of flowers and on their return renamed the property the Engadine Estate. Their home, too, was surrounded by wildflowers – waratahs, Christmas bush, Christmas bells, flannel flowers and native rose. Waratah Street was named by McAlister because it passed through a grove of waratahs. Mrs McAlister speculated in land while her husband, Charles, was involved in local community matters and was a councillor of the first Sutherland Shire Council. McAlister served on the council until 1914 but died the following year. Mrs McAlister later entered a business partnership with W R Ainsworth, a resident of Engadine and shire president, and continued to live in Engadine for some years before moving to Cronulla.

Around 1900 McAlister subdivided part of his land and there was also a release of Crown Lands in 1906 and 1910 and gradually families began to settle in the area. Early families included the Pooles, Coopers, Higgersons, Heggertys, Hanlons, Nolans, Prestons and Trinders. Sergeant Nolan had retired from the police force at a young age owing to an injury and had a farm where he kept goats imported from Switzerland and cultivated 7,000 strawberry plants. The Hanlons owned a property on the corner of the highway and Station Street and Mrs Hanlon was one of the first women to receive a horticultural degree from the Hawkesbury Agricultural College. John Higgerson had been a jockey and was noted for his honesty. The family had moved from Bottle Forest and two of the sons were the only

The Princes Highway at Engadine in 1928, looking south. (Government Printer)

Engadine men to serve in World War I. Wally Higgerson later became a ranger at the National Park and died at the age of 74 years in 1955.

In that early period there were no amenities, although milk was delivered by Wellman of Bottle Forest (Heathcote), residents walked to the shops at Heathcote for supplies.

There was an early one-horse coach service operated by a former railway worker, named Cooper, which carried four inside and two outside with the driver. The coach met the train at Heathcote and passengers paid weekly. Prestons opened a general store on the Princes Highway, opposite Station Street, in 1921 and it also operated as post office, newsagent, butcher and baker. The meat was delivered daily to the store by train.

Engadine's first school was a shed behind this store. Many veterans of World War I settled in the area and streets were named Amiens, Anzac and Bullecourt. Following this tradition there is also Tobruk and Villers Brett.

Residents of Anzac Parade who arrived in 1916 were Mr and Mrs A W Bower. Mr Bower was discharged from the army because of war wounds. He became the Captain of the local bush fire team and served from 1916 until 1942 and then served in World War II. He was succeeded by his son, Walter. The Bowers operated a produce store from 1932 until 1942.

The residents agitated for a railway station and formed the Committee of the Engadine Platform League but were forced to finance it themselves and a quote of £380 was received from the Railway Department. Mrs McAlister contributed £200 of this amount and was asked

to name the station. The opening of Engadine Railway Station on Saturday, 20 November 1920 was a gala occasion. However the station was not a permanent stopping place and there was no booking office. During the day a green tin disk, attached to a pole, was used to stop trains and in the night there was a lamp with a lit candle to halt the evening train.

A 1924 map of the district notes an area between Engadine and Heathcote on the south eastern side of the railway as having "fine views of Ocean". Frank Cridland when writing about the Old Illawarra Road and the Pass of Subugal notes:

The first half-mile of the road towards the ford [the Pass of Subugal] already is assuming the appearance of a village street, as it is the frontage of a number of scattered houses in the newly christened village of Engadine, which until recently was part of the township of Heathcote.

Cridland also notes the cairn of stones known as the Bottle Trig Station and Engadine Creek which has its source in a peaty tableland near Heathcote. It ran through the park close to Engadine Station and about a mile downstream drops over the spacious Engadine Falls.

The Engadine post office opened in 1927 and a local public school was finally built and opened in September 1932. By then unemployment, as a result of the depression, began to ease but in that year a settlement of unfortunate unemployed workers and their families settled at Engadine.

In 1931 an official ceremony was held near

the Engadine Reservoir for the "turning on of the water" but this was only a low level water scheme and mostly supplied Sutherland. There was not a good water supply until the completion of the Heathcote Reservoir in 1954. In 1933 there was a population of 417 and 111 dwellings.

Four Engadine men died during World War II: Reg Sladden was killed in Greece in 1941; Doug Buckle, a member of the Air Force, died in Greenland as a result of wounds; Ronald Back, a leading seaman, died in 1945 after telegraphing his family from Western Australia that he was on his way home, he was washed overboard in heavy seas 12 hours out of Melbourne; Wally Bostock, a Japanese POW died while being transported with other prisoners in a Japanese troopship.

By 1947 Engadine had 295 dwellings and a population of 1,203. By the mid 1950s Engadine was developing with a picture theatre planned. New shops and a baby health centre were built as well as a new post office and telephone exchange.

In the 1960s vacant Crown land in the Heathcote – Engadine area was subdivided for housing and Engadine became part of the growth of Sutherland Shire.

Yarrawarrah is the Aboriginal name for the mountain ash (*Eucalyptus regnans*), one of the largest of the gums with lovely creamy or grey bark. In the timber trade it is called Australian oak. The name Yarrawarrah applied to a nearby ridge, Yarrawarrah Heights, along which the Illawarra railway line runs. Today's suburb is located between Engadine and Loftus. The area was vacant Crown land and was subdivided in the 1970s.

Father Dunlea and Boys Town

Father T V Dunlea was born in Roran, County Tipperary, Ireland in 1894 and ordained a priest in Wexford in 1920. He was appointed parish priest to Sutherland in 1934 and soon after became concerned about the care of young boys. In 1939 the priest leased a cottage on the corner of Flora and Glencoe Streets, Sutherland and placed under the care of a matron three boys. The cottage was unfurnished and had few facilities but boys kept arriving. There were complaints about the bad drainage and overcrowding. Sutherland council was forced to serve a minor nuisance notice on the home and threatened to close it unless drainage was improved and the number of inmates reduced. The local health officer, W L Cooper, donated £1 to Boys Town stating he had "the highest respect for the work Father Dunlea is doing". Father Dunlea then established a tent village in National Park at Loftus and held a protest march through the streets of Sutherland with the boys carrying banners bearing the signs "We are the Australian Refugees" and "Give Us a Fair Go".

In July 1940 a public meeting called for assistance in the care of the boys and subscriptions were made to enable the purchase of 90 acres of land. Subsequently land was purchased at Engadine once owned by the Higgerson family. John Higgerson, known as "Honest John", had been a jockey famous for his riding skill and honesty who lived at Bottle Forest (Heathcote) but in c. 1899 moved to Engadine. The Premier of New South Wales, A Mair, laid the foundation stone of the settlement on 4 May 1941, but buildings were already being constructed and some 40 boys were in residence.

Boys Town was capable of housing some 150 boys aged between nine and 15 years (in 1954 there were 110 boys at Boys Town) and the establishment contained its own school and also taught trades such as bakery, butchering, carpentry and boot repairing. In addition there were other facilities such as gardens, playing fields, shops and a hospital. A Macquarie Street doctor donated his services to Boys Town. The town was self sufficient, and also supplied their own vegetables and eggs.

Boys Town protest march from their camp near Loftus to the streets of Sutherland. Banners read, "We are Australian Refugees", "Give us a fair go" and "Australian Homes for Australian Lads". Father Dunlea is in the centre.
(Sunday Telegraph, 28.7.1940)

Boys Town was non-denominational and was inspired by the American Boys Town, founded by Father Flanagan. It catered for neglected, orphaned, unmanageable or delinquent boys including those recommended by the Children's Court for a probationary period. In the 1950s it was estimated some 41% of the boys had been before the courts. At Boys Town the boys elected their own mayor and eight aldermen who were responsible for welfare and discipline. The council also had the power to act as a tribunal to impose penalties for misdemeanours. The De La Salle Brothers conducted the schooling, training and supervision of Boys Town from c. 1942 and the aim was to provide a healthy lifestyle, both mentally and physically.

Father Dunlea was devoted to the work of Boys Town and it was said it became a crusade for him. He believed "There is no such thing as a bad boy". He was a familiar figure often riding around the district on horseback and then, later, in a yellow roadster. His generosity was well-known and during the depression he was said to give the shoes from his own feet to one in need. Father Dunlea also established a home for alcoholics at Loftus. He remained principal until his retirement in 1951 when, in 1952, the Archbishop of Sydney, Cardinal Gilroy, appointed the Society of Salesians of Don Bosco to operate Boys Town. Modernisation of the buildings was then carried out and by 1970 it was estimated some 2,000 boys had passed through Boys Town. Boys Town is supported by public subscriptions and contributions from parents and guardians of the boys. Father Dunlea died on 22 August 1970 and is buried at Boys Town.

Menai and Bangor

Owen Jones, an early settler, hailed from Bangor, Wales and arrived in the area in 1895 naming it for his birthplace. However, far away in Tasmania there was another area named Bangor and the postal authorities later believed this confusing and changed the Sydney area to Menai in 1910. Again, though, it retained a Welsh connection being named for the Menai Straits between the Isle of Anglesey and Bangor in Wales. Jones's first dwelling was a rough bush shelter but he later built a weatherboard house, which became the first post office. On Christmas Eve, 1976, this cottage, dated as c. 1896, was destroyed by fire. It was believed arson was responsible.

By the early 1900s Bangor – Menai was a small settlement of poultry and vegetable farms somewhat isolated as Sutherland was some five miles distant. It was not an easy life for the market gardeners as they had to get their produce to the markets in Sydney. To achieve this meant an overnight journey. A resident of the area, Fred Midgley, some years ago wrote a word

A City Man's Home. This substantial weatherboard dwelling, in close proximity to the Cronulla -Sutherland tramline, was featured in a 1911 edition of Australian Country Life *. It was described as the property of a city businessman. (Australian Country Life, 1911, Mitchell Library)*

picture of the journey these farmers undertook. He disclosed the farmers mostly travelled in pairs and departed from their farms around 8.30 in the night transporting their produce to the Lugarno Ferry and travelling through the night to arrive at the markets in the early hours of the next morning. Saturday was the main market but other market days were Tuesday and Thursday.

At that early period roads were bad, clouds of dust in dry weather, but worse in wet conditions when it was possible to become bogged and the farmers had carts packed with produce – cabbages, turnips, peas, beans, passionfruit and peaches packed in cases, 100 cases to the ton, and after crossing the river, the Lugarno Hill on the Hurstville side was always difficult. The carts had no brakes and a pole had to be inserted in a wheel as a brake. After crossing the river the carts followed Forest Road from Hurstville and joined the Wollongong Road at Arncliffe and on to the city.

To keep the produce fresh lettuces where placed in split chaff bags suspended under the carts and fastened at four points. Imagine their delight on arrival at the markets with produce and where peaches reached two and sixpence a case. The farmers breakfasted at the markets where they could obtain tea and toast for threepence. However, their work was not over once they sold their produce. On the way home they had to purchase supplies such as flour, sugar and tea at Redfern, Newtown or Hurstville. There were also blacksmiths in Hurstville where they could have their horses shod. Midgley points out that later, after the Woronora River Bridge opened in October 1912, they took their

The Lugarno ferry crossing the Georges River, c. 1910. This service, established in 1843 when Mitchell was building the Old Illawarra Road, was the first ferry service over this part of the Georges River. It was not until the mid 1890s when Menai (formerly called Bangor) was settled by farmers that the service was used regularly. (SPF, Mitchell Library)

horses to Sonny Bennet at Sutherland. Much of the timber used by the local blacksmiths and wheelwrights came from the ironbark forests.

The Midgley family were pioneers of Menai, Richard Midgley having arrived in 1896 when he and his family were the second settlers to take up residence. Their first home was a bush hut of poles covered with sheets of turpentine bark. The washing was done in the creek and later a two room weatherboard house was built. Mrs Fanny Midgley started the first school in her home which nine local children attended. She

also operated a Congregational Sunday school in her home from 1901 and a small church was built in 1906. Richard and Fanny's grandsons, twin brothers Alfred and Fred Midgley, were foundation members of the Sutherland Shire Historical Society and enthusiasts of the history of Menai and the Woronora River. They contributed to the knowledge of Sutherland Shire with their many booklets and articles. Another pioneer was Granny Dawson, who died in 1936. It was said she had still used her petrol iron, kerosene lamp, and primus stove for cooking.

In the early 1900s the district was affected by a major drought when all the local crops failed. The locals existed by cutting the "grass tree gum" which was sent to Sydney where it was used in the manufacture of varnishes, stains, lacquers and munitions. They were hard times and children's clothes were made from calico flour or sugar bags. The wild bees nests were robbed, for wax and honey which was strained through firstly a hessian, then a calico bag. Honey was sold for one shilling for a four gallon tin and bees wax reached three shillings a pound.

By the outbreak of World War I, Menai was very much a rural community with orchards and poultry farming, although there was a factory manufacturing gut rope near the home of a local carpenter, named Bentley, off the Old Illawarra Road. The gut was obtained from Stone's slaughter yard in Bexley and was stretched out between trees, then twisted by hand and rubbed down with rasps and sandpaper. The gut was used in the drives of sheep shearing machines.

In 1951-1952 bush fires ravaged parts of Sutherland Shire and there was also a shortage of water. By 1954 Menai was in danger of being without water and there was agitation for piped water supplies. At that time there was a decision made that Sydney was to have a nuclear reactor and the site chosen was Lucas Heights, between Menai and North Engadine. Around the same period the eastern area of Menai was subdivided and named Bangor so Owen Jones's original name was perpetuated.

By the 1970s Sutherland council had initiated, with other State and federal departments, plus statutory authorities and private landowners, an overall plan for the development of housing in the Menai area with five centres at Alfords Point, Bangor, Illawong, Lucas Heights and Menai. The idea was to create a satellite city capable of housing 60,000 residents in good living conditions with a variety of dwelling styles for a broad socio-economic group. The first subdivision was in 1975 and by 1977 blocks of land were selling from $15,000 with top prices of $25,000. There were to be all facilities plus public reserves and community land. The scheme also included traffic distribution with a system of town collector and distributor roads. Even the street names were planned with those of Alfords Point having botanical significance, Bangor with Aboriginal names, Illawong of historical nautical origin, Lucas Heights has Australian pioneers, and Menai has famous Australians, including sports people.

Illawong was once known as East Menai but it was renamed in the 1960s. The Aboriginal name means "the land between two rivers" – the Georges and Woronora Rivers. Early development occurred in the 1880s when wealthy businessmen from Sydney built holiday homes in the area, which was accessible by boat from Como. Near Fowler Road and Bignell Street, Robert Fowler of the Fowlerware Pottery built Cranbrook, which was later owned by Sir James Joynton-Smith, who became Lord Mayor of Sydney in 1918. He was also a founder of *Smiths Weekly*, which operated from 1 March 1919 until 28 October 1950. There was little residential development in the district until 1980 when the first subdivisions occurred.

Lucas Heights Atomic Reactor

The area of the suburb of Lucas Heights was part of the 150 acre grant made to John Lucas in 1825. Lucas was born in the colony and has been described as "miller, builder, publican and political activist". He established his water mill close to the river but it was destroyed by fire in the 1830s. Lucas's son, also named John, was born in 1818 and elected to the Legislative Assembly in 1860 as the member for Canterbury. In 1864 he won both Canterbury and Hartley but chose to sit for Hartley. He was said to be a scathing critic of governments whatever their political complexion and hated waste and bungling. He was interested in Sydney's water supply and advocated the damming of both the Georges and Warragamba Rivers. Lucas was one of the first to visit Jenolan Caves and it was through his efforts that the caves were opened to the public and declared a reserve. The Lucas Cave, which was discovered in 1860, was named in his honour.

In the early 1950s the Australian Atomic Energy Commission made a decision that Sydney was to have Australia's first nuclear reactor and their choice for the site was Lucas Heights. On 29 December 1954, at the Sutherland council chambers, a conference was held to discuss the site which the council had already decided was to be used for a sanitary dump. The commission had selected the area because it was remote but accessible by road and had availability to electricity and water. The council agreed to move the sanitary depot further west, with the approval of the army authorities, who held the land. After various discussions with experts in the field the council agreed there would be no objection to the establishment of the reactor at Lucas Heights.

The reactor was to be isolated on a plateau south of Menai. Menai was the closest settlement with ironbark trees still lining its streets. According to the *Daily Telegraph* in 1958, the residents were not unduly perturbed about the establishment of the reactor. It was stated they were more worried about when water would be laid on to their homes or whether their hens were laying. They trusted the experts that there was no danger to Menai and saw that the project would mean water for their poultry farms.

The natural bush was bulldozed, construction commenced and Lucas Heights, operated by the Australian Atomic Energy Commission, opened in 1957. General Stevens, who was chairman of the commission, declared the facility "would not be used for destruction, for military purposes". It was a research facility with a programme of research in development of nuclear power, the utilization of radioisotopes for medicine and other associated fields, directed towards the long-term development of the resources of the country. A major part of the work was towards the development of a high temperature gas cooled reactor system (HTGCR). The establishment was to allow the training of personnel in all aspects of atomic energy relevant

to Australia's needs. The reactor at Lucas Heights is a slightly modified version of the British DIDO, rated at 10 MW (heat), has a maximum flux of 101^4 neutrons per cm^2 per second, uses heavy water as moderator and primary coolant and ordinary water as secondary coolant, passing through cooling towers.

In 1986 the Australian Atomic Energy Commission was reconstituted as the Australian Nuclear Science and Technology Organisation (ANSTO). They operated one of the laboratories at Lucas Heights and the second was operated by the CSIRO.

The suburb around Lucas Heights expanded and the district was no longer a remote area and by the 1980s concerned local residents had formed an action group against the establishment and called for its removal. The suburb itself was renamed Barden Ridge.

By March 1997 there was more concern when it was disclosed the federal government was considering building a waste reprocessing plant at Lucas Heights. The plant was to deal with the storage problem for 1,600 spent fuel rods from the reactor, reprocessing them in Australia rather than overseas.

It was envisaged Australia's experimental "Synroc" technology for immobilising nuclear

Situated 35 kilometres south of the centre of Sydney, the Lucas Heights nuclear reactor began operations in 1958 when the surrounding area was bushland. Today it is surrounded by recent housing developments. There are five reactors similar to this around the world, three have been decommissioned, one refurbished and one in Denmark is unchanged. (Sydney Morning Herald, 4.9.1997)

waste be used which would demonstrate its first commercial use, particularly to the nuclear power industry in the Asia-Pacific region. After reprocessing, the waste would still require burial "somewhere in outback Australia". It was stated the proposal was in the "early stage of consideration". In April 1997 a toxicologist, Dr Michael Selley, and a former senior federal government official stated that Australia does not need the Lucas Heights nuclear reactor and could save $1 billion over the next decade by closing it. He claimed nuclear medicine needs could be imported far cheaper than producing them at Lucas Heights. Dr Selley had joined the campaign against a new reactor as well as the proposal for a nuclear waste re-processing plant at Lucas Heights. A Cabinet submission has recommended the construction of a new reactor at Lucas Heights but Sutherland Shire Council and mayors from surrounding municipalities have campaigned against the proposal.

In May 1997 Dr Gordon Thompson, Australian born and director of the US Institute of Resource and Security Services Studies, claimed a new reactor at Lucas Heights would give the federal government the expertise to build atomic weapons and claimed the government wanted the reserve capacity to build the weapons if necessary for emergency defence. He further stated Australia should seriously consider moving it (the reactor) from Lucas Heights. Dr Thompson advises nations on nuclear issues.

In September 1997 the federal government announced that almost $300 million was to be invested in a new reactor at Lucas Heights.

Following protests by politicians, environmentalists and local residents, it was pointed out that alternative sites were not suitable because of the half-life of the radiopharmaceuticals which would be produced. They need to be near an airport so there is no deterioration of the product in the time of transportation. Sutherland's mayor, Kevin Shreiber, demanded a senate inquiry into the new reactor.

Bundeena

On the shores of Port Hacking and surrounded by Royal National Park is the tiny settlement of Bundeena, once known as Jibbon Village Reserve. Land was granted here in 1823 to Owen Byrne who acquired some 400 acres. On 5 November 1863 George Simpson, who had been employed by Thomas Holt, purchased 50 acres at Cabbage Tree Point. His son built a large house on the waterfront, with attics in the roof, named Tyreal House, later Tyrell. It became a licensed hotel, Simpson's, and was popular with honeymooners.

The first official guide to National Park of 1893 states:

The water beneath Pulpit Rock is deep and limpid, and the firm bottom of sand many feet below the surface is the haunt of shoals of fish visible in thousands. This is a favourite resort of visitors to Tyreal House (best known as

Simpson's Hotel) on the rising slope hard by, and of course it is accessible from the water. Private selections were secured, before the Park was dedicated, on the shore line between the Yarmouth Estate and the opposite point to Warumbul on the South-west Arm.

South of Simpsons the source of Cabbage Tree Creek is described as:

a tiny rill, which grows in width and volume on its way to the sea, and finally expands into a large and deep basin nearly a mile in length and half that measurement in breadth. The lagoon is fringed with groves of exquisite cabbage palms and tree ferns, a beautiful sheet of water amidst lovely surroundings.

Simpson is remembered in the naming of Simpsons Bay. In 1916 permission was granted for a ferry passenger service to operate from Simpsons Hotel to Gunnamatta Bay. Visitors to the hotel came from the Sutherland train by horse drawn vehicle to the wharf at the foot of Port Hacking Road to be ferried across to Simpsons Wharf.

Earlier it was said the Aborigines crossed the water hereabouts and certainly around Bundeena there are rock carvings. On Jibbon Head or Port Hacking Point on a large flat rock the Aborigines made outlines of fish, wallabies and men. The La Perouse Local Aboriginal Land Council suggests the six fingered male figure may represent one of the mythical spirits described in the stories of the coastal Aboriginal people. Beached whales provided abundant meat but the whale engravings in the area may also refer to a local story telling how the first people arrived using a large canoe belonging to a whale. There are some 80 Aboriginal sites around Port Hacking (Aboriginal "Deeban") and it is possible the Dharawal people lived here for 30,000 years or more. Around 1918 Harry Simpson, who was a boatshed proprietor, while blasting rock on his land, exposed part of a cave where Aboriginal bones and stone weapons were concealed.

In the 1880s Jibbon Village Reserve became the Yarmouth Estate which was owned by the Reform Land Investment and Building Company. The company planned to mine for coal in some 2,000 acres adjoining Jibbon Village Reserve. However the coalmining operation was halted by an appeal from a strong anti-coalmining opposition in State parliament appealing to the attorney general.

The 1893 official guide to National Park states:

A road was cut from Garie Beach in the South to Jibbon Beach in the north, traversing the whole ocean frontage of the Park, and from this main thoroughfare, branch roads were made to near Costen's Point, to the Spit, and to near Wentworth's Fountain, all of which terminate on the bank of Port Hacking.

In 1924 Frank Cridland recounted a gruesome tale. On 9 July 1904 a vessel, the *Nemesis*, was lost on the Jibbon Bombora and some six weeks after the event Cridland and a friend were fishing towards Boat Harbour when they thought

Simpson's Hotel (originally known as Tyreal House) was a popular holiday destination, located on Simpsons Bay. Visitors could reach it by travelling to Little Turriel Bay by coach, and cross to the southern side of Port Hacking using the regular boat service that operated from the 1880s until about 1920. Only the foundations (re-used for a ranger's cottage) remain. The Norfolk Island pine tree is still there. (Australian Country Life, 1911, Mitchell Library)

they saw a whale spouting. A closer examination revealed the hugely swollen body of man which they surmised was a sailor, only just been released from the foundered vessel. A few days later the body was washed onto Jibbon Beach and buried unidentified.

On 1 January 1935, G H Mobbs and Son, auctioneers of Parramatta, offered "Absolute Water Frontages adjoining National Park, opposite Cronulla" at "The Cream of Port Hacking Jibbon Beach Estate, Bundeena". The terms were from £3 per lot deposit, the balance £1 per month with interest at 5%. At the time Captain Ryall was the proprietor of the ferry service when the popular *Myanbla* plied the route. Captain Ryall later moved to Tuross Lakes and died in 1955.

The auctioneers also offered for private sale choice camp sites, building blocks and farmlets from £15 each lot with a £1 deposit and ten shillings per month, with interest at 5%.

Even in the 1950s Bundeena, an Aboriginal name meaning "noise like thunder", was described as an "idyllic little township ... as yet

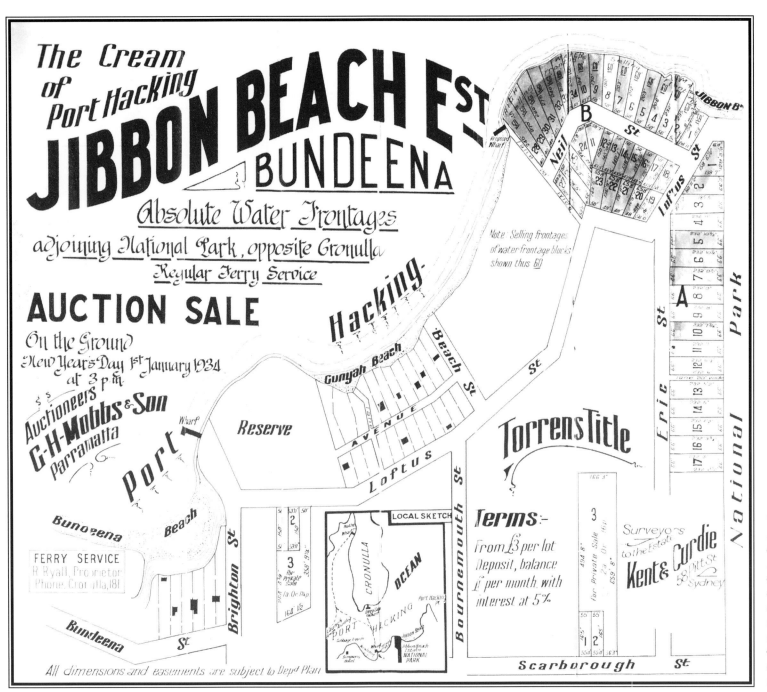

This plan from 1 January 1934 shows development at Bundeena since the 1920s when there were only a few scattered dwellings. Frank Cridland commented in the 1920s that the little village, on the edge of the National Park, was in danger of becoming a "struggle town". (Kingsclear Books)

quite unspoiled". A R C Phillips writing of the area in 1952 declared:

there was but one made road, one motor car, and not more than two motor trucks. There is a post office which is also a general store and cafe, a butcher's shop, an ironmonger's where fishing gear is prominently displayed, and of all things, a frock shop!

On weathered sandstone cliffs a few old humpies existed where itinerant fishermen enjoyed their solitude.

The area is a starting point for many lovely walks within the Royal National Park and the ferry trip from Cronulla to Bundeena is part of the excursion. Enthusiastic bushwalkers enjoy the Bundeena, Marley, Wattamolla, Garie walk where the track follows the sheer sandstone cliffs above the sea and winds through coastal heath. Some prefer the plateau walk from Bundeena Wharf via Brighton Street to Yarmouth Swamp, which recalls the old estate name. A fire trail leads to Jibbon Trig which rises 285 feet, while another leads to the northern headland of Marley Beach. Along the route one may see carvings by the Aboriginal people who once roamed the area.

Heathcote

Heathcote straddles both the Princes Highway and the southbound railway line and was named by Major Mitchell for an officer, one of two brothers, who had served with Mitchell under the Duke of Wellington during the Peninsular Wars (1809-1814).

The district was noted for its fine timber, including red cedar, ironbark and turpentine. Soon after the survey of the Illawarra Road, people were anxious to take up land. In 1843 George Hall made an application to purchase 50 acres and accordingly, Major Mitchell in a minute dated 20 July 1843 instructed his assistant surveyor, Mr Darke, "to take an early opportunity of laying out Bottle Forest in such allotments as may seem expedient in view of the prospective importance of the situation, taking

Roadworks in Heathcote, corrugation on gravel, October, 1928 (GPO, Mitchell Library)

care that the allotments fronting the road should be of limited area". Hall is believed to have built a "guest house" close to the Illawarra Road but it soon closed. The name Bottle Forest appears on a map c. 1843 made by Mitchell's son, Roderick and an area marked out in the shape of a soldier's early water bottle. Another forest to the south was named for the surveyor – Darke's Forest.

Heathcote Hall
In the 1880s a wealthy brick maker, Isaac Harber, acquired the freehold of 50 acres, the Heathcote Hall Estate. Here he built a fine home, Heathcote Hall, c. 1887 with grounds in the style of an English manor. (Kingsclear Books)

Darke's survey laid out 14 town allotments from seven to 31 acres and among those who took up land in 1845 was Patrick Hynes who acquired lots 19 and 17, of 30 and 24 acres, in June and October. Others who acquired land were George Coulson, a licensed victualler of Sydney, W T Fleming, E M Hill, John Annan and Peter Caffray.

In 1865 Thomas Holt also acquired 41 acres at Bottle Forest. It was here that Holt had over 300 dingoes destroyed after they had played havoc with his flocks of sheep.

In 1846 there was a population of 15 adults in four dwellings. However the district was extremely isolated and although the soil was good it would have been difficult to get produce to market and Bottle Forest was abandoned in the 1860s.

The fine forests still attracted the timber getters and bullock drivers. Some stoic men in the 1860s eked out a living collecting native honey, cutting railway sleepers, oyster gathering, fishing or charcoal burning. One, Matthew "Matty" Keough is credited with growing the first tobacco in the district.

In 1886 the Illawarra railway line opened to Waterfall, and Heathcote Station, called Bottle Forest during construction, also opened. In 1883 the colonial secretary had been unsure about the rail route through Bottle Forest and had considered a line through the Hacking River Valley with easier grades and a shorter route. An official enquiry found the Bottle Forest route less costly and although the colonial secretary believed his route would give easy access to the National Park, there was access from Waterfall.

In the 1880s a wealthy brick maker, Isaac Harber, acquired the freehold of 50 acres, the Heathcote Hall Estate. Here he built a fine home, Heathcote Hall, c. 1887 with grounds in the style of an English manor. Local red cedar was used for the fittings in the interior of the Victorian style mansion which had a large central tower overlooking the countryside. Harber was also involved with the construction of Sydney's Imperial Arcade and only enjoyed Heathcote Hall briefly before heavy financial losses necessitated him to try and dispose of the property. It passed to the mortgagees and then to the Financial Institution but during the 1890s depression they were unable to sell the estate. It was then arranged that George Adams, who had started the Tattersall's lotteries, arrange a lottery with Heathcote Hall as the first prize, valued at £7,000. The property was won by a Sydney builder, S Gillett, who said he had only two "pleasurable sensations" from the win: one when he was notified he had won and the other when he disposed of the estate five years later but for much less than its valuation. Heathcote Hall is listed by the National Trust of Australia (NSW).

Waterfall and Heathcote National Park

Waterfall was named for two waterfalls not far from the railway station, the upper with a drop of 14 metres, and the lower with a drop of 39 metres, on Waterfall Creek. Major Mitchell laid out the Illawarra Road from Engadine towards Waterfall and near Engadine relics of the convicts and a convict built baker's oven have been discovered dating from the road's construction. Major Mitchell reported to the governor that he constructed his Illawarra Road along the crests of the ranges and pointed out that the road did not cross a single watercourse.

Waterfall is a small suburb, some 40 kilometres from Sydney, on the Princes Highway and leads to the Lady Carrington Drive within the National Park. Waterfall was noted for its clear mountain air which caused the area to be selected for the establishment of the Hospital for Consumptives in 1909. A horse bus operated from Waterfall to the hospital but was replaced with a truck in 1918. The truck had a canvas top and "slit sides" but was also later replaced with a 1934 International bus known affectionately as "Old Biddie".

The section of the Illawarra railway, Sutherland to Waterfall, opened on 9 March 1886 and included the branch line to Loftus.

Waterfall celebrated its centenary in 1986. The original Waterfall terminus was a half mile south of today's station and there were few facilities. There was a loop to allow the engines to change ends necessitating the locomotives to return to Sydney, tender first, at a reduced speed. With the completion of this section of the line, Hurstville then had 16 terminating trains, Sutherland two and a further two to Waterfall. Only one operated to Waterfall in 1907. In 1890 the Waterfall line was duplicated and the station relocated 16 chains north of the original terminus. In 1905 a new marshalling yard, island station platform and small locomotive depot were constructed in conjunction with extensive deviations to ease grades between Waterfall and Coalcliff. Traffic was heavy on occasions necessitating the use of two turntables at Waterfall. The steam locomotives took on coal and water at Waterfall and to have a constant supply of water, a dam was constructed on Heathcote Creek. Later with the use of diesel trains, Waterfall was less important but is being used again with the haulage of coal to the loader at Port Kembla.

The Como railway camp closed in mid 1885 and moved to Heathcote and Waterfall but it was an isolated life for the railway workers and their families. They would not have envisaged the many bushwalkers who come to enjoy the area, particularly the 2,250 hectares of Heathcote National Park, formerly Heathcote State Park, accessible from both Heathcote and Waterfall.

The area of mainly Sydney sandstone, with rugged ridges and deep gullies, consists of heathland and woodland vegetation with eucalyptus, blackbutt, bloodwood plus a wide variety of shrubs with both the grass tree and Gymea lily. The wildflowers are spectacular during spring. The park is associated with the noted conservationist Myles Dunphy who first explored the Heathcote valley when he was only 17 years old in 1908. Inspired by the area's beautiful and wild nature, Dunphy became an ardent fighter during the late 1920s and early 1930s to have lands declared recreational reserves. Dunphy studied the national park systems of the USA and their problems, obtained their booklets and passed them on to others, including government officers.

In 1914 Dunphy, with others, formed the Mountain Trails Club for members to enjoy bushwalking but, more importantly, to have a conservation aim. There had been earlier bushwalking clubs but Dunphy pioneered pack-carrying walks and the famous Paddy Pallin began manufacturing hiking equipment in 1930. During the 1920s the Mountain Trails Club fought against abuses in the National Park and, with the Sydney Bushwalkers, pioneered conservation and educational objectives. Myles Dunphy named many of the features in Heathcote National Park and with his sons, Milo and Dexter, built the trail along Heathcote Creek from Yellow Pool to the Causeway.

In 1935 the Mountain Trails Club obtained a lease of 100 acres in the Heathcote Valley which was finally made part of Heathcote Park in 1962. The Boy Scout organisation also obtained leases, the St George Association held over 100 acres in 1932 in Heathcote, and another lease was obtained at Waterfall, now known as Camp Coutts. It was hoped to retain the whole of Heathcote Creek as a primitive area. An area of 1,760 acres was gazetted in 1943 for public recreation and the following year the name Heathcote Primitive Area adopted. In 1945 it was re-gazetted for the preservation of native flora and fauna. In 1963 the size of the park increased to 3,900 acres and later extended south to the Woronora Dam road, creating an area of 5,560 or 2,252 hectares.

Garrawarra Hospital, Waterfall

The staff of Garrawarra Centre for Aged Care are proud of their establishment's long history. Sue Rosen has published *A History of Garrawarra Hospital* in which she tells the interesting and early beginnings of the hospital.

Tuberculosis is a disease caused by several species of *Mycobacterium*, collectively called the tubercle bacillus. Tuberculosis in humans is usually caused by the human and bovine varieties of the bacillus (*M. tuberculosis* and *M. bovis*), respectively. It was the plague of the 19th century, featured in various novels and even the opera *La Traviata*.

The disease steadily declined in the 20th century except during periods of war and national catastrophe. Once long sea voyages and

removal to mountain climates were recommended as a cure.

As Rosen points out, in Sydney sufferers of the disease were once treated in asylums for the poor, with men being sent to Liverpool and women to Newington. However the area of Waterfall was noted for its clear air and in 1909 the government decided to establish a hospital to specifically treat patients with tuberculosis. An area of 1,135 hectares was set aside and the plan also included a cemetery.

The Hospital for Consumptives, designed by

Government Architect, Walter Liberty Vernon, opened on 14 April 1909 and 230 male patients were transferred from the Liverpool Asylum. It was 1912 before accommodation was provided for women when an area of 120 beds opened. The hospital was self sufficient with an area for cultivating vegetables, an orchard, and a pig and poultry farm. In 1914 the establishment became Waterfall State Sanatorium for Tuberculosis and was the principal hospital in New South Wales for the treatment of the disease. Some patients were incurable and there was some debate as to

The Waterfall State Sanatorium for tuberculosis in 1951 cared for TB sufferers. It later served as a hospital for the chronically ill and aged. (GPO, Mitchell Library)

whether they should be housed with patients hopeful of making a recovery as it was felt they "undermined the spirit" of those taking the rest cure. Treatment recommended was "light, sunshine, fresh air, rest when necessary, and graduated exercise, diet, and contented minds, with a determination to improve". In addition, within the hospital grounds there were graded walks which patients were encouraged to follow.

In 1918 extensions were carried out at the hospital including the construction of a number of two-bed open-air chalets. The following year Waterfall Sanatorium had reached the status of the largest sanatorium in the State with accommodation for 565 male and 223 female patients. In 1923 Sir James Kingston Fowler declared:

A Sanatorium is not an institution it is an atmosphere. The right system no doubt stands for a great deal, but the man at the head of it stands for far more. He must feel that he is an apostle, an evangelist, that he has a message to deliver and be filled with a desire to deliver it. The less time he spends in administration and the more he spends in preaching the gospel and inspiring his patients with a new hope in life, the better.

During the 1920s more remodelling was carried out including the transformation of the former dining room into an open ward. In 1921 there were 376 patients in residence at the beginning of the year reaching a total of 556 for the full year. Of that number 59 were rated as "(Arrested) Quiescent" or inactive; 107 as much improved; 147 as improved; 67 as unimproved

and there were 190 deaths. In 1930, of 509 patients, 20 were inactive; 60 much improved; 175 improved; 94 unimproved and there were 103 deaths.

The 1930s saw a shortage of beds for, despite the fact that tuberculosis was in decline, Waterfall was accepting advanced chronic cases and the dying. The patients who were improving were able to work in the carpentry shop or in the vegetable garden. The hospital continued to serve tuberculosis patients until 1957 when some 100 patients were still in residence. A method of early diagnosis had been introduced following World War II with regular chest X-rays and patients were transferred to Randwick Chest Hospital while some were permitted to be out-patients.

There was some conflict as to what role the Waterfall Sanatorium would fulfil but finally the suggestion of State Member of Parliament, Rex Jackson, was adopted. He had campaigned for a hospital for the aged and chronically ill. He named the hospital Garawarra, a name inspired by pioneer conservationist, Myles Dunphy for Garawarra Park, deriving from the Gara Estate and "warra" from the name Illawarra. It is said the spelling "Garrawarra" was a bureaucratic mistake which annoyed bushwalking clubs associated with the formation of Garawarra Park. The Garrawarra Hospital functioned from 1958 until 1991 as a hospital for chronic diseases and diseases of the aging. A services review and master plan for the hospital in 1991 resulted in another name change in 1992 to Garrawarra Centre for Aged Care. It functions as a multi-purpose aged care centre specialising in dementia, rehabilitation respite and day care services.

Royal National Park

Royal National Park is Australia's oldest national park, having been dedicated on 26 April 1879. It has always claimed to be the world's second oldest national park after Yellowstone in the USA. However, the National Parks and Wildlife Service points out Yellowstone was established in 1872 but "it was not officially designated as a National Park in legislation until 1883, four years after its Australian counterpart".

In the 1870s a number of men in public life called for government to provide public parks, pleasure grounds and places of recreation close to heavily populated areas in New South Wales. They considered these were essential for the good health and vigour of the populace. The Premier of New South Wales, Sir John Robertson (1816-1891) developed the idea of establishing a "national domain for rest and recreation". The area he selected was south of Port Hacking, with an ocean frontage, "and comprising sections in the parishes of Sutherland, Heathcote, and Bulgo, and the whole of the Crown lands within the parish of Wattamolla". The country covered 18,000 acres. In 1880 the park was increased to 36,300 acres and it now covers 15,014 hectares.

On 31 March 1879 the land was reserved from sale and on 26 April dedicated as a reserve

Visitors to Audley alight from a boat on the Hacking River and are met by a horse drawn vehicle. A regular ferry service ran between Cronulla and Audley for many years. (Mitchell Library)

Girls on Freshwater River, 1914. These visitors to the National Park pose rather stiffly for the camera beside the Hacking River, above the causeway. This section of the river was, at this time, called "the Freshwater". (GPO, Mitchell Library)

for "the use of the public for ever as a national park". Sir John Robertson was one of the original trustees.

In the 1880s timber getters had felled timber in what was later the national park area, particularly near Garie where much of the cedar was cleared. Garie had been an early private selection with land cleared in the 1830s. Even in 1900 horses, sheep and cattle grazed behind the beach. During World War I permission was again given for timber to be cut within the park. In 1921 a further agreement was made for the park's timber to be used by a coal mining company, with two sawmills to be built within the park. A conservation society took out a court injunction against the firm and prevented this intrusion to the park.

Obviously the prime consideration for the park was for people's pleasure not as an area for the preservation of the environment and native flora and fauna. In 1885, 160 acres of land on the shores of Port Hacking was cleared for a deer park enclosed by a high fence. Seven fallow deer were presented by the Trustees of Parramatta Park, and E S Cox, (a descendant of William Cox who built the road over the Blue Mountains) of Fernhill, Wallacia presented five "valuable" red deer but they broke free and roamed the entire park. In 1893 Sambar deer were brought from the Philippines and some Javan rusa deer from the Timor Islands, which had come to Australia via New Caledonia, possibly in 1907 when a shipment was in Sydney en route to New Zealand. By the late 1960s it was believed there were approximately 1,000 deer within the national park.

Hiring boats at Audley, 1947. Allambie House is above the boat shed. Until World War II this was a busy holiday guest house. As private transport improved, day trips to Audley became the norm. When it was no longer used for overnight accommodation, Allambie House fell into disrepair and was demolished in 1975. (GPO, Mitchell Library)

Some friendly kangaroos, possibly on Lady Carrington Drive. The 1893 Guide to the National Park noted that such were the beauty spots along this road that "they should not be left unseen". (Mitchell Library)

The *Official Guide to the National Park of New South Wales* 1893 points out that 12 years before the Illawarra railway was built, the area "14 chains" south of Sutherland Station "to the precipitous descent upon Port Hacking River commencing immediately beyond Loftus terminus, was covered with wild scrub, containing good, bad and indifferent timber". At the end of December 1883 the National Park trustees had some 80 acres of Loftus Heights cleared by contract but "all good shade, well-grown and handsome trees, Christmas bushes, waratahs, gigantic lilies, plants and shrubs of an ornamental nature should be left intact". By 1885 some 230 acres had been cleared and the following year some 2,000 acres was "dealt with".

A "via militaris" for military manoeuvres, claimed to be the equal of any such ground in the Southern Hemisphere. It was constructed from Loftus Junction to Loftus Heights with provision for military signalling to St Leonards, Middle Head and outer South Head of Port Jackson, to Waverley, to Randwick, to Bare Island, the shores of Botany Bay, Jibbon Beach and to the ocean, with Flagstaff Hill as the principal signalling station.

A carriage way was built from Sutherland to Loftus and an avenue of trees planted between the park gate and Loftus Junction. From 1886 to 1890 annual encampments of "our infantry, mounted infantry, cavalry, and field artillery forces" were held on Loftus Heights. Personnel, stores, field guns and horses were carried to the camp by rail. After Federation in 1901, and the formation of the Commonwealth Military Forces, training at Loftus diminished. However,

the area was still used by the New South Wales Field Artillery until shortly after the outbreak of World War I in 1914.

In 1864 Lord Audley, attached to the surveyor general's department, surveyed much of the area making an accurate survey of the river. He camped near the junction of the Hacking River and Kangaroo Creek.

After the establishment of the park, this area became known as Audley, one of the park's most popular spots. Lord Audley married Emily, a daughter of Surveyor-General Sir Thomas Mitchell in 1857. By 1893 it was stated that Audley was "so popular as a holiday and recreation resort" that the trustees had to enlarge and improve the original pavilion with a large dining room, apartments and sleeping accommodation for 22 guests. Another cottage was built at Warumbul and a cottage, with board room for the trustees, at Audley, as well as a slip and shed for hauling and repairing boats, boat-houses, carpenter's shop, smithies and stables. A concrete weir was constructed at Audley but earlier there had been a flood gate, worked by block and tackle.

The Lady Carrington Drive was completed in 1886, named for and opened by Lady Carrington, the wife of the governor, Baron Carrington (1885-1890) and claimed to be the most beautiful drive in the world. In the first six miles from Audley, 15 brooks were crossed and they were given the Aboriginal names of various Australian birds such as "Dirijiri" for the wagtail, and the creeks were spanned with rustic bridges. In 1892 two stone basins were placed beside the road to take water from a spring beneath the

hillside and both were named for the then governor, the Earl of Jersey. The trustees considered the road "without doubt ... the greatest thing the Trustees yet have done in opening out the Park". They also realised that National Park contained an infinite variety of beauty which should be "preserved in its natural state". In 1902 dingoes could still be heard in the park but the trust believed it was not their function "to nurture or foster the growth of these pests" and native cats or snakes were not to be tolerated.

During the 1920s National Park was a popular escape area for Sydneysiders and boating a pleasant pastime. On the Hacking River there were four-oared vessels with colourful sunshades for gliding languidly on the river. As the motor car increased in popularity, the park was even more accessible and areas like Garie became a landscape of tents at weekends. In 1932 Garawarra Sanctuary was included in National Park, including the open forest above Werrong.

Originally, simply National Park, following the visit of Queen Elizabeth II in 1954, in 1955 it was proclaimed Royal National Park. In 1967 the park came under the control of the National Parks and Wildlife Service.

Generations of Sydneysiders have visited and enjoyed National Park and bushwalkers tramped the many trails within the park to Bundeena, Marley, Wattamolla or Garie. Marley is dangerous for swimming but a feature of the area are the sand dunes and behind them the swamp and lagoon which attracts fauna and the wide variety of birds. Wattamolla is popular as a family picnic area with good swimming. In 1796 the bay here was named Providential Cove by explorers Bass and Flinders in the *Tom Thumb* as it provided them shelter. Garie is said to be Aboriginal for "sleepy" and is a popular surfing beach. From Garie a coastal walk leads to Burning Palms, the Figure 8 Pool, Palm Jungle and, for the enthusiastic walker, Otford.

The early citizens who had the foresight to call for the preservation of National Park, bequeathed to Sydney a magnificent area of varied and spectacular scenery with grand coastal cliffs, idyllic beaches, deep cut valleys of rainforest, streams and tidal rivers where visitors enjoy quiet bushwalks or follow various activities such as swimming, boating, bicycle riding, camping, fishing or surfing.

In January 1994 Royal National Park was a victim of the disastrous bush fires which ravaged many parts of Sydney, particularly Sutherland Shire. Many people in Sydney were shocked to witness on television screens the extent of the damage and the suffering of animals and creatures within the park. Some 12,000 hectares of Royal National Park, which for so many years had been part of Sydney's heritage, was burnt. Rangers and other organisations, such as WIRES, rallied to give assistance to the injured wildlife and plan for the park's recovery.

Terror of Bushfires

For Australians, even those living in cities, bushfires are a natural part of the Australian scene. During the winter months the authorities often burn off large areas in the hope of preventing disastrous fires during the summer months. Nevertheless, periodically there are bushfires destroying national parks, forests, people's homes and threatening lives, and they receive Australia-wide, and even overseas, coverage by the news media.

In 1939 bushfires in New South Wales were so extensive that a public outcry called for improved methods for the prevention and fighting of fires. It was estimated damage was over £1 million and 182,450 acres of forest were burnt.

Sutherland Shire, with its huge expanse of bushland, and Royal and Heathcote National Parks, has often suffered from bushfires. In the summer of 1901-1902 there were very high temperatures and 1902 was said to be one of the driest summers on record. There were some ten settlers, with their families resident in the area of Bangor, and the local creeks had dried up. During December 1901 disastrous fires raged unchecked for three days around the district with

Black Saturday, 14 January 1939, when fires burned around Sydney. This Sylvania woman watches her house burn. (Kingsclear Books)

strong north-east winds swinging to north-west winds. The summer of 1951-1952 brought fires throughout the State, said to be worst for 40 years. They caused a great loss of property in Sutherland Shire on 15 and 16 December. That month a film night to aid victims of the bushfires was held at an open air theatre in Bellingara Road, Miranda. Many were homeless as some 40 to 50 residences in the shire were destroyed.

Local poultry farmers suffered excessive losses because of the extreme heat and it was estimated 33% of poultry in the shire died and there was a consequent drop in egg production. Winds blew at 60 mph and a sudden change of wind swept the fire towards the small village at Grays Point where ten houses were destroyed in a few minutes. Some were angry as they felt the fires had originated in National Park on Crown land. There was a call for a 100 foot firebreak between National Park and residential areas. Some 60% of National Park had also suffered damage. The fires pointed out weaknesses in bushfire fighting organisation and a group captain was appointed to co-ordinate brigades and volunteers.

As a result five new bushfire brigades formed, making 11 in the shire, and the council chambers became the fire control centre. In January 1952 fires struck again, particularly at Engadine, Sutherland and National Park. Seven houses, four temporary dwellings and one fibro house were destroyed. Engadine, which itself had suffered, raised £1,792 for relief of victims.

Menai was a dangerous area, particularly in 1954 when they suffered severe water problems. Poultry farmers were forced to cart water, some 6,000 gallons a week. Finally on 4 September

A poster issued by the Royal National Park to help control bushfires. (GPO, Mitchell Library)

1954 the Heathcote-Engadine High Level Water Extension was turned on by the Water Board. At that time it was estimated there were 1,800 bushfire brigades manned by about 45,000 volunteers in New South Wales.

In January 1965 fierce fires raged through National Park and the Bundeena Bushfire Brigade faced a wall of fire on Bundeena Road. The fire threatened hundreds of homes and great tracts of National Park were burnt. During fires in 1980, five bushfire fighters died while fighting fires near Loftus.

All Sydney was shocked by the extent and devastation of the fires of January 1994 when

some 70 bushfires encircled Sydney on various fronts causing the loss of four lives and damage estimated at $50 million. Sutherland Shire was particularly affected.

Within the shire, one woman died, many people were hospitalised, 104 homes destroyed as well as a church and school. Some 5,000 residents were evacuated and 25 square kilometres of the shire blackened. As Sydney tuned to radio and television, the shock was enormous as homes at Bangor, Como West and Bonnet Bay were lost. The fires swept from Sandy Point to Alfords Point and to Illawong in 15 minutes and at the same time Como was an inferno. A firebug was blamed for the fire which jumped the Old Illawarra Road and the Alfords Point Motorway.

By 3.30 pm on Saturday 8 January, as the *St George and Sutherland Leader* was later to report "the fire was boiling and created a huge cell of flammable gases above the Woronora River. The cell exploded showering Bonnet Bay, Como West and Jannali with superheated air and embers". The Heathcote Bushfire Brigade rushed through blazing bush to rescue a family trapped at Como and saved a man and his two daughters but a woman had died and was floating in a swimming pool. There was an inferno at Bundeena and for many residents it was a "weekend of hell".

Cronulla-Sutherland Sharks

Rugby league commenced in Sutherland Shire with the formation of the Sutherland Junior Rugby League Football Club, in 1912-1913. It was the second oldest junior club in the State and was founded by a local barber, Jim Brady. The team played in a paddock, later Robertson Street, Sutherland. Some of the club's members fought in World War I and the war, the influenza epidemic and the depression had their

effect on the club. A new club formed in 1920 and played at Waratah Park but by 1931 had moved to Sutherland Reserve. Because the area was close to Woronora Cemetery, the team became known as the "Grave Diggers".

Following World War II one of the great names of rugby league, Norm Provan, was associated with the club and played for Sutherland and Australia. The Sutherland club produced many first grade players including Col Rasmussen, Bobby Bugden and Steve Rogers, the latter two also representing Australia. In 1987 the Sutherland club celebrated their 75th Anniversary.

The Cronulla-Sutherland Sharks rugby league team was one of the youngest teams in the premiership in New South Wales. In 1952 a group of players formed a junior team, Cronulla-Caringbah, and played in the St George competition. In 1963 the team entered the Sydney Second Division (the inter-district competition) and played in the Grand Final but were defeated, 9-7, by Kingsford.

In 1967 the club became Cronulla-Sutherland and entered the Sydney premiership. Soon after an English player, Tommy Bishop, came to Australia to become captain-coach of the team. In 1970 Bishop was Player-of-the-Year. Bishop persuaded a fellow player from his former English team, Cliff Watson, to also come and join the team in Sydney and they are credited

The Sharks have been active in donating funds to the Sutherland Hospital Caringbah. Money raised in their leagues club has gone towards the refurbishing of wards. (Sutherland Hospital Caringbah)

with improving the play and spirit of the team so that it played in the Grand Final in 1973 which was won by Manly. Unfortunately for the team, the following season Bishop went to Brisbane as player-coach, and Watson to Wollongong. Cronulla-Sutherland again dropped in the competition.

Since the inception of the junior team the club faced problems financially and even in the early period it seemed as if it would be forced to close. A leagues club complex was commenced at Endeavour Field, the team's home ground, but there was insufficient money to complete the project. Finally the government, the NSW Rugby League and loyal fans saved the Cronulla club.

Johnny Raper was a coach to the club and in 1978 Norm Provan joined the team and that year the Sharks again reached the Grand Final. They lost the match on a re-play to Manly-Warringah. The team, with colours of blue, black and white, had a number of representatives with the Australian Test team, Steve Rogers, Greg Pierce, Steve Kneen and two New Zealand brothers, Dane and Kurt Sorensen.

The well-known coach, Jack Gibson joined the Sharks and in 1988 was succeeded by Alan Fitzgibbon. That year Andrew Ettingshausen and Mark McGaw made their Test debuts. Ettingshausen, with 111 tries, was to hold a record for the most tries in a career; the most tries in a season, with 18 in 1994, and the most tries in a match with 5 in 1989. In 1989 Gavin Miller won every major individual prize, including the Rothmans Medal and Dally M Award. In 1990 both Ettingshausen and Mark

McGaw played with the Kangaroos tour of Britain and France.

Arthur Beetson, who once owned the Como Hotel, was also, for a period, a coach to the Sharks team. In 1994 Ettingshausen was again selected as a Kangaroo and for a second time scored 5 tries. His 18 tries for the season was a Sharks record. In the 1990s the former Australian Test representative, Steve Rogers, saw his son, Matt, also play for the Sharks.

During the 1990s the format of rugby league changed with the formation of Super League, under which Cronulla-Sutherland now plays. In 1997 Super League and the RSL joined forces for the staging of a rugby league Anzac Day Test between Australia and New Zealand at Sydney Football Stadium. Selected for the team were two Cronulla players, David Peachey and Andrew Ettingshausen.

Rugby League Grand Final at Sydney Cricket Ground in 1978. Cronulla was defeated by Manly. (St George and Sutherland Shire Leader)

Kurnell Oil Refinery

The Caltex Oil Refinery by night, c. 1970.
(Sutherland Shire Council)

Captain Cook would be amazed to sail into Botany Bay today. Not far from where he landed at Kurnell in 1770 is the oil refinery and soaring overhead the aeroplanes from Kingsford Smith Airport. Both Kurnell and the landing site stand in the shadow of the oil refinery which had its origins in the 1950s.

Over the mangrove and tidal areas of Woolooware and Quibray Bays was built the Captain Cook Drive to serve the Caltex Oil Refinery. Mangroves live between the sea and land on sheltered shores in bays, estuaries and the lee of offshore islands. Some 30 species are found in Australia and offer a sheltered marine environment suitable for crabs, whelks, shrimps, prawns, barnacles, isopods and amphipods. Insect, nectar and pollen eating birds are usually found in mangroves and mangrove snails feed on algae and other material. The new roadway was built only to the entrance to the refinery and the road to the village and historic site, in the 1950s, remained in a poor condition.

In 1951 the Caltex Oil Company approached Sutherland Shire Council concerning establishing an oil refinery at Kurnell. Initially there was public dismay and consent was refused but by 1952 the objection was withdrawn. The first construction was the building of the Captain Cook Drive by Sutherland Shire, at an estimated cost of £163,659 (on a cost-plus basis). AOR requested a Federal Aid Grant to be paid to the council to be used for the new road. The road was completed in mid 1954 at a cost of £181,456. The first sod had been turned by Premier J J Cahill at the Cronulla end, leading from Elouera Road, on 28 February 1953. The refinery was to cover some 174 hectares and a heavy transport road was required. Australian Oil Refining Pty Ltd, was a subsidiary of Caltex Oil and construction on the refinery commenced in December 1953. Some 3,000 men were employed on the project. The scrub was cleared, swamp areas drained, water and sewerage facilities provided and the refinery itself constructed. On completion the refinery employed 670 people, the majority of them residents of Sutherland Shire. The refinery was one of the largest in Australia and was capable of refining 19 million litres per day.

In 1985 the refinery had a name change from Australian Oil Refining Pty Ltd to CRL (Caltex Refinery Co Pty Limited). By the early 1990s there were over 100 storage tanks at the refinery with a capacity from 500,000 barrels of crude oil to less than 10,000 barrels for refinery fuel oil tanks.

In 1963, close to the Caltex Refinery, the Australian Oil Lubricating Refinery (ALOR) commenced production of special grades of lubricant oil based stocks and greases.

A still from the film Forty Thousand Horsemen *showing the immensity of the Kurnell sand dunes before they were mined.* (National Film and Sound Archive)

Other firms were attracted to the outskirts of Kurnell and included Abbott's Laboratories, manufacturers of pharmaceutical products and Carbon Black and Phillips Imperial Chemicals. The latter closed in the 1980s due to a downturn in the economy.

As early as the 1870s a Noxious Traders Association was formed and one member of parliament, Alfred Fremlin, suggested a special noxious trades site be established. Following a Royal Commission in the 1880s a bill was finally passed in 1886 to provide for the resumption of 1,500 acres at Kurnell, together with Crown land, for the noxious trades site covering 3,570 acres at the entrance to Botany Bay. In the 1920s a portion of this site from Cape Solander to Boat Harbour was withdrawn from sale, leased and renamed Endeavour Heights. Kurnell was once a weekend retreat, although during the depression a "Happy Valley" settlement was established, mainly accessible only by the La Perouse ferry. Even in the 1940s it was almost pioneer territory with local Stan Latta operating his bus services along the rough road and urging passengers to get out and push when the bus was bogged in the famous "Cudgery Hole". By the 1970s attractive and modern homes were built and the Commonwealth government purchased the Towra Point wetlands and reserved the area as Towra Point Nature Reserve.

In March 1987 the *Sydney Morning Herald* commented:

The park area was also improved for the celebration of the bicentenary of Cook's arrival in 1770. The sign says 'Welcome to Kurnell, the birthplace of a nation', but there is nothing welcoming about the oil refinery, the LP gas plant, the brick works, the sandmining scars, the smell of sewage or the unofficial rubbish tips and rusted mechanical hulks that line either side of Captain Cook Drive.

There was a call for a large scale, clean up of Botany Bay and the Kurnell Peninsula. The people of Kurnell also expressed opposition to the zoning of toxic chemical industries and local residents formed the Kurnell Action Committee in November 1985.

The committee opposed the toxic zoning on the grounds of degradation of Australia's birthplace and risk to the unique flora and fauna. The zoning area was directly adjacent to the Towra Point Nature Reserve which was already under stress from oil spills and industrial waste. In 1988 the committee was celebrating victory when toxic industry was banned from the area and a national park area, with the Towra Point Reserve, declared covering 1,400 hectares. Sandmining companies on the peninsula were also too close and heavy industry was encouraged to move away. In addition a long battle against Bayer Australia Ltd, who had made application to operate a plant in the area, was won when they put their Kurnell buildings up for sale.

In 1997 Sutherland Shire Council rejected plans for a major resort on the Kurnell Peninsula but it is still on the "drawing board". In addition there were a number of major developments mooted including more sandmining, an upgrade to sewage treatment works and an electrical co-generation plant for the Ampol petroleum refinery.

Sutherland Shire 2000

Sutherland Shire grew, from the time of white settlement, with the construction of Mitchell's Illawarra Road and the Illawarra railway. Small settlements developed but in 1900 Sutherland was still an isolated area, although the area's first newspaper, the handwritten *Sylvania Post*, appeared that year. The pioneering days were then in the past and Connell, Laycock and Thomas Holt figures of historic note.

When the Sutherland Shire was inaugurated in 1906 the population was estimated at 1,500. By 1920 Como was being advertised in the *Smith's Weekly* as "The Coming Suburb" with opportunities to acquire land with a £2 deposit and Sutherland Shire had more subdivided land than occupied properties in that decade. By 1924 the new Georges River Bridge was completed, the first major project undertaken by a local council, and the longest road bridge in New South Wales.

The shire was still rural in character with orchards and numerous poultry farms. The residents of Sutherland Shire were disconcerted by the lack of town water and in 1920 a local member stated the localities of Sutherland, Miranda and Cronulla had a population of 5,000 and might soon grow to 10,000. In fact the

Cronulla Shopping Centre, 1964. Cronulla Street had a diverse range of shops and plenty of traffic at this time. In the succeeding years the nature of this area has changed dramatically and it is now dominated by cafes, restaurants and bargain shops. In 1988 the northern part of the street was transformed into a pedestrian mall. (GPO, Mitchell Library)

population did reach 10,000 in 1928 but by the end of the 1920s only 123 houses had town water. The residents had to wait a number of years for the for the first stage of Woronora Dam to be commenced. A Parliamentary Standing Committee on Public Works concerning the proposed scheme of water supply for the shire of Sutherland was held in 1921 with numerous local personalities, such as C O J Monro, appearing as witnesses. Even in the 1940s the number of vacant lots was almost twice the number of existing houses scattered over the subdivided area of Sutherland Shire.

The greatest growth in Sutherland Shire occurred following World War II when streets of new houses appeared. The 1950s was a period of general prosperity. It was a time when the whole economy changed to a credit basis. Previously to borrow was difficult and most believed irresponsible and a social sin. Jobs and incomes were secure and there was full employment. Also motor cars were accessible to families and became almost a necessity. It also meant the development of suburbs beyond public transport. It resulted in drive-in picture theatres and self-contained shopping centres. The car also changed the design of suburban homes as a garage became a necessity and was often attached to, and later integrated, into the design of a house. By 1961 71% of Sydney's private dwellings were owner-occupied. *The Daily Telegraph* of 13 March 1965 carried an advertisement proclaiming "Now You Can Join the Smart Young Families Heading for HEATHCOTE". By the 1970s there were boom areas to the south of Sydney and the establishment of several regional shopping centres.

The Royal Australian Institute of Architects proclaimed most of the houses in the newer residential areas as "basically conventional in their planning and construction, but their architectural expression encompasses the full gamut between 'dull' and unashamedly 'featurist'." However it was noted the expansive views and challenging sites found near the waterways stimulated architects to design some houses which "respond to and enhance the local environment in which they are built." The RAIA noted several homes in the Sutherland Shire in a publication of 1971 – *444 Sydney Buildings*: 12 and 14 Boronora Parade, Lugarno; 7 Kangaroo Point Road, Sylvania designed by Edwards, Madigan & Torzillo, 1961; Port Hacking Road & Pembroke Street, Sylvania designed by Bill Lucas in 1953 and noted as one of the first good post-war houses in the area; 89 Dolans Road South, Burraneer Bay, Ancher, Mortlock & Murray which won the Sulman Medal, 1960. Also noted were 344 Woolooware Road South, Burraneer by Bowe & Burrows, 1961; 733 Port Hacking Road, Dolans Bay, Romberg & Boyd, with McConnel, Smith & Johnson, 1967; and 67a Lilli Pilli Point Road, Port Hacking, by Harry Seidler, 1963, which won the Wilkinson Award 1966.

As well, public and industrial buildings were recorded: St Anne's Church of England, Como, 1965, by Hely, Bell & Horne; Ferguson's Garden Centres Pty Ltd, at North Sylvania 1967 by Devine, Erby & Stowe; the Sylvania Waters development of 1960; Sutherland Shire Soccer Football Club by Hely, Bell & Horne 1966; the AOR Oil Refinery at Kurnell by AOR refinery engineers Impressive, engineering design of a refinery complex; Kirrawee High School, by the NSW Government Architect, 1966; the Methodist Church at Caringbah by Loder & Dunphy. 1958; and the Atomic Energy Research Establishment 1960, 1962 and 1964.

In 1966 Sutherland's population was 134,058, ten years later 156,688 and at the census of 1991 184,399. Residents of today's Sutherland Shire live in a scenic area with the advantages of accessible waterways and natural areas such as Royal National Park.

They have recreational, cultural and educational facilities the pioneers would never have envisaged. The 19th century suffered pollution from noxious industries, from dirty streets, no garbage collection, from the many horses, and disease-carrying flies and insects, which resulted in various diseases such as the typhoid epidemics late in the century.

Today pollution is still evident but it takes different forms with pollution of the waterways, traffic congestion, and for Sutherland residents, a concern about the only atomic reactor in Sydney and threats of increased noise levels from decisions concerning a new Sydney airport. Nevertheless, few would relinquish the pleasures of living in Sydney's largest shire by moving to less favoured places. They would probably agree with the *Australian Country Life* of 1911 which declared "The charm of the district, from the residential point of view, is its convenience to town and the lovely views to be obtained from pretty well any part of the district".

Origin of Names and Suburbs – Sutherland Shire

Alfords Point - Early settler, James Alford held 50 acres of land in the area.

Audley - Named for George Edward Thickness-Touchet, 21st Baron Audley, colonial surveyor, who established a camp in the area in 1863-1864. Audley made the first accurate survey of the Hacking River and later became a son-in-law of Sir Thomas Mitchell. Audley was disinherited and his two unmarried daughters lived and died in genteel poverty.

Bangor - The original name for Menai given to the area by early settler, Owen Jones, who was born in Bangor, Wales. To avoid confusion with an area similarly named in Tasmania, the postal authorities renamed the area Menai. In the 1950s the eastern area of Menai was subdivided and named Bangor.

Barden Ridge - Originally Lucas Heights, the area was renamed for an absentee landlord named Barden who earlier held land in area.

Birniemere - Part of Kurnell and originally land covered by Alpha Farm owned by Captain James Birnie in 1815.

Bonnet Bay - Area named by the Geographical Names Board, NSW Lands Department, 1969, for a geological feature, a headland and cave said to resemble a colonial woman's bonnet.

Burraneer - Named by Surveyor Dixon in 1827 during his survey of the area. Said to be of Aboriginal origin meaning "point of the bay". Dixon used numerous Aboriginal names in the area.

Bundeena - Of Aboriginal origin meaning "noise like thunder".

Caravan Head - On the southern shore of the Georges River. The Geographic Names Board has no record of the origin of the name.

Caringbah - Originally the district was Highfield. The name change occurred when the Sutherland - Cronulla steam tram service commenced in 1911. Caringbah is said to be the Aboriginal name for the small marsupial, the pademelon or red-necked scrub wallaby. It is also said to be a corruption of the Aboriginal name.

Como - Named for Lake Como in Italy by James Murphy, who had been manager of the Holt-Sutherland Estate. Murphy established the Como Pleasure Grounds.

Cronulla - The Aboriginal name was Kurranulla "a place of pink sea shells". The beach was noted for its "pippies", a pinkish coloured bivalve. In 1827 Surveyor Dixon named the area the Cronulla Beaches.

Dolans Bay - Named for Patrick Dolan who held land there from 1856.

Engadine - Charles McAlister purchased land here in 1890. After visiting Europe with his wife, McAlister named his property the Engadine Estate for the Engadine district of Switzerland, noted for its hills and valleys of flowers.

Grays Point - Two origins exist. One for Samuel William Gray who owned land on the point; the second version is that it was named for a resident ranger of National Park, John Edward Gray, a local identity and resident of Gundamaian.

Gymea - Named for the giant Gymea lily (Doryanthes excelsa) by the government surveyor, W A B Greaves in 1855 because of the prevalence of the plant.

Gymea Bay - Named from the same source as Gymea.

Heathcote - Named for Thomas Mitchell during the construction of the Illawarra Road for an officer with whom Mitchell had served during the Peninsular Wars (1809-1814).

Holtmere - A name used on the first map of Sutherland Shire covering an area of Kurnell held by pioneer, Thomas Holt.

Illawong - Originally East Menai. Name changed when a public school was established in 1960. Of Aboriginal origin meaning "the land between two rivers", the Georges and Woronora Rivers.

Jannali - Aboriginal origin meaning "moon" or "beautiful moonrise". Named with the opening of the railway station in 1931.

Kangaroo Point - On the southern shore of the Georges River. The Geographic Names Board has no record of the origin of the name.

Kareela - Named in 1968 and of Aboriginal origin from "kari-kari" meaning "fast", probably for the area's strong south winds. Alternatively also said to mean "place of trees and water". Originally the area was called Salisbury.

Kirrawee - Once known as Bladesville from the Blade family who were early residents of the district. When the railway station opened in 1931 the suburb became Kirrawee, Aboriginal for "lengthy". Formerly the area had been part of Sutherland.

Kurnell - Said to be an English version of an Aboriginal name "Collonel" but usually accepted as a corruption of the name of early settler, John Connell who acquired land in 1821.

Lilli Pilli - In 1868 Robert Cooper Walker mentioned a "small point called Lilli Pilli" for the local myrtle trees (Acmena smithii). The fruit of the tree (in autumn and winter) is edible with a sour, refreshing flavour, although coastal specimens eaten by the Aborigines are small and tough. In the Illawarra area the Aboriginal name was "Tdgerail".

Loftus - Named for Lord Augustus Loftus, Governor of New South Wales (1879-1885).

Lucas Heights - Named for early settler John Lucas who established a water-driven mill at the head of the Woronora River in 1823. Renamed as Barden Heights.

Maianbar - On the southern shore of Port Hacking adjoining Royal National Park, it was originally two subdivisions, Fisherman's Bay Estate, offered for sale in 1927, and Sand Spit Estate offered in 1929.

Menai - Once the district of Bangor named by Owen Jones in 1840 for his birthplace in Wales. To avoid confusion with Bangor in Tasmania changed to Menai in 1910. Named for Menai Straits between Wales and the Isle of Anglesey.

Miranda - Named by James Murphy, one time manager of the Holt-Sutherland Estate as he felt the name "euphonious, musical and an appropriate name for a beautiful place". Said to be chosen from the character in Shakespeare's play, The Tempest.

North Engadine - The northern area of the McAlister estate, named for the Engadine district of Switzerland.

Oyster Bay - Named for the abundance of oysters found in the bay and appeared on the map of Surveyor Wells of 1840. A pioneer of the oyster industry in the area was Ernie Edwards, who had an oyster farm on the shore of the bay.

Point Solander - Named by Captain Cook for Dr Carl Solander during the Endeavour voyage of 1770.

Point Sutherland - Named by Captain Cook for the Orkney seaman, Forby Sutherland who died and was buried at Kurnell during the Endeavour voyage of 1770.

Sandy Point - Named for locality. The Sandy Point Estate formed in 1925 with every lot having a water frontage. Developed from 1950s.

Sutherland - Various theories as to name. Once called Southerland. One version is that area named for Cook's seaman, Forby Sutherland who died at Kurnell; another that it derived from the Parish of Southerland, proclaimed in 1835; and another that when the Illawarra railway station opened it was named for the Honourable John Sutherland, NSW Minister for Works, 1860-1872.

Sylvania - Named by James Murphy, founder of Como Pleasure Gardens, because of the sylvan nature of the area.

Sylvania Waters - Derived from the suburb of Sylvania with the development of the canal estate in Gwawley Bay.

Sylvania Heights - Derived for the area above Sylvania and along Kangaroo Point Road where waterfront lots were available in 1919. Area developed from 1950s.

Taren Point - Once Comyns Point, then Cummins Point and Commons Point, perhaps for a local resident, but origin unknown. Once weekenders and fishing huts and first residential development in 1911 with a ferry commencing services in 1916.

Waterfall - Named for waterfalls near railway station. Became a railway depot with the opening of the Sutherland-Waterfall railway line in 1886.

Wattamolla - Aboriginal name meaning "place near running water". Named as a civil parish in 1835.

Woolooware - Named by Surveyor Dixon in 1827 and given an Aboriginal name meaning "a muddy flat". Originally mangrove swamps in the area but reclaimed for various parks and playing fields, including Endeavour Field.

Woronora - In 1827 Surveyor Dixon chose a name "Wooloonara" meaning "place of no sharks". Later Woronora said to be Aboriginal name meaning "black rock".

Woronora Heights - Derived from Woronora and approved by Geographical Names Board in 1985.

Yarrawarrah - Aboriginal name meaning "place of echoes".

Yowie Bay - Various versions. Said to be Aboriginal for "place of echoes" but also once Ewey or Ewie Bay. Ewe is a female sheep and Ewey or Ewie said to be the Scots name for a ewe's lamb. In Yorkshire, England "Yow" is a female sheep and "Yowie" is the baby lamb. Thomas Holt employed both Yorkshire and Scots shepherds. Said the inlet on the Hacking River was where Holt's ewes gave birth to their lambs, hence Yewie or Yowie Bay.

Bibliography

Alanson, A G, *Kurnell, The Birthplace of a Nation*, George B Philip & Son, 1933

Andrews, Malcolm, *ABC of Rugby League*, ABC, 1992

An Official Guide to The National Park of New South Wales, 1893

Australia's Yesterdays - A Look at Our Recent Past, Readers' Digest, 1974

Australian Country Life, Sutherland Shire, 25 September 1911

Australian Dictionary of Biography, MUP

Australian Encyclopaedia, The Grolier Society of Australia, Sydney, 1965

Australian Railway Historical Society Bulletin, June 1948

Baker, Anthony, *What Happened When - A Chronology of Australia from 1788*, Allen & Unwin, 1992

Beasley, Margo, *The Sweat of Their Brows, 100 Years of the Sydney Water Board, 1888-1988*, Water Board, 1988

Benson, Doug & Howell, Jocelyn, *Taken for Granted, The Bushland of Sydney and Its Suburbs*, Kangaroo Press, 1995

Blanche, H, *The Story of Australia*, North York Publishing Co

Boyd, Michael, *Woronora Cemetery & Crematorium Sutherland, 1895-1995*, Cemetery Trust, 1995

Carey, Gabrielle & Lette, Kathy, *Puberty Blues*, McPhee Gribble - Penguin Books, 1979

Cashman, Richard & Meader, Chrys, *Marrickville, Rural outpost to inner city*, Hale & Iremonger, 1990

Cobley, John, *Sydney Cove, 1788*, Angus & Robertson, 1962

Concerning Heathcote Hall, Bottle Forest and Heathcote District, 1926

Cridland, F, *Port Hacking, Cronulla and Sutherland Shire*, Angus & Robertson, 1924

Curby, Pauline, *Cronulla Public School, The Early Years*, Cronulla Printing Co

The Daily Telegraph 11.11.1924; 11.10.1957; 26.4.1958; 4.11.1996

Daily Telegraph News Pictorial 15.11.1927

Dawes, J N I & Robson, L L, *Citizen to Soldier, Australia Before the Great War, Recollections of Members of the First AIF*, MUP, 1978

District News, 28 June 1956

Dyster, Barrie, *Servant & Master, Building and Running the Grand Houses of Sydney 1788-1850*, UNSW, 1989

Eryldene E G Waterhouse National Camellia Gardens, Gordon

Fairley, Alan, *Along the Track, A Guide to the Bushland Around Sydney*, 1974

Fairley, Alan, *The Beaten Track, A Guide to the Bushland Around Sydney*, 1972

Fitzgerald, Shirley & Keating, Christopher, *The Urban Village, Millers Point*, Hale & Iremonger, 1991

444 Sydney Buildings, RAIA, Angus & Robertson, 1971

Freeland, J M, *Architecture in Australia, A History*, Penguin, 1968

Geeves, Philip & Jarvis, James, *Rockdale, Its Beginnings and Development*, Rockdale Council, 1986

Geographic Names Board

Hatton, Joan and Muir, Lesley, *The Triumph of the Speculators*, Southern History Group, 1984

Hilferty, Kevin, *Sutherland, Australia's Birthplace*, Sutherland Shire Council, 1986

Hughes, Robert, *The Fatal Shore*, Collins Harvall, 1987

Hutton Neve, M, *A Short Authentic History of Cronulla*, Southland Historical Press, 1970

Hutton Neve, M, Article - *Bundeena Township*

Hutton Neve, M, *Martha Matilda of Sydney Town*, Sutherland Shire Historical Society, 1972

Hutton Neve, M, *The Early Days of Kurnell to Cronulla*, Sutherland Shire Historical Society, 1972

Hutton Neve, M, *The Hon Thomas Holt, MLA*, Southland Historical Press, 1970

In and Around Sydney with the Steam Tram, Book 3, NSW Steam Tram and Railway Preservation Society

Jibbon Aboriginal Rock Engravings Walk, Pamphlet - National Parks & Wildlife Service

Journal of Arthur Bowes Smith: Surgeon 1787-1789, Australian Documents Library, 1979

Journals and Letters of Lieutenant Ralph Clark, 1787-1792, Australian Documents Library, 1981

Journals of the House of Commons. Testimony to the House of Commons Committee on the Return of Felons, Vol 37, pp 309-11

Kennedy, Brian & Barbara, *Sydney and Suburbs, A History and Description*, Reed, 1982

Kirby, David R, *From Sails to Atoms, First Fifty Years of Sutherland Shire, 1906-1950*, Sutherland Shire, 1970

Kurnell Action Committee pamphlet

Kurnell, Birthplace of a Nation, Shire Pictorial Publications, 1969

Lawrence, D.H., *Kangaroo*, Penguin Books, 1954

Leisure in Sutherland Shire, Sutherland Shire Council

Mackie, Robert D, *Pacific Portal Pictorial Cavalcade*, Souvenir of Sutherland Shire

Macquarie, Lachlan, Governor of NSW, *Journals of His Tours in NSW and Van Diemen's Land 1810-1822*, Trustees of the Public Library of NSW, 1956

McDonald, Helen, *A Walk Around Sutherland*, Sutherland Shire Council, 1990

Mahony, Dennis, *Botany Bay, Environment Under Stress*, Charden Publications, 1979

Manly Daily, 14.5.1997

Mathews, Phillip, *Sutherland, Birthplace of a Nation*, Currawong Press, 1977

Midgley, F, Heathcote, *The Beginnings*, Sutherland Shire Historical Society

Midgley, F, *Illustrated History of the Sutherland Shire, Birthplace of a Nation*, Southland Historical Press, Sutherland, 1969

Official Guide to the National Park of New South Wales, The Trustees, 1914

Organ, Michael, *Illawarra and South Coast Aborigines 1770-1850*, Aboriginal Education Unit, Wollongong University, 1990

Phillips, A R C, *Bundeena*, Savings Weekly, 18 September 1952

Pigeon, Rhys, *Miranda*, Sutherland Shire Historical Society Journal

Pollon, Frances, *The Book of Sydney Suburbs*, Angus & Robertson, 1988

RAHS Journal, Vol 10, 1924; No 69, May 1968; Vol 72, October 1986;

Robinson, Les, *Native Trees of Sydney*, The Gould League

Roe, Jill, ed, *Twentieth Century Sydney, Studies in Urban and Social History*, Hale & Iremonger, 1980

Rosen, Sue, *A History of Garrawarra Hospital*, 1993

St George and Sutherland Shire Leader, 11.1.1994; 5.11.1996

Salt, D F, *Gateway to the South, First Stop Sylvania, An intimate insight into the origins of Sutherland Shire*, 1987

South Coast Illustrated Tourist Guide, 1924

Spearritt, Peter, *Sydney Since the Twenties*, Hale & Iremonger, 1978

Spearritt, Peter and Poulsen, Michael, *Sydney A Social and Political Atlas*, Allen and Unwin, 1981

Stewart, David, ed, *Investigating Australian History, Using Evidence*, Heinemann Educational Australia

Sun - Herald 16.8.1981

Sunday Telegraph, 28.7.1940; 27.4.1997

Sutherland Rugby League Football Club - article, 1987

Sutherland Shire Historical Society Bulletin, Stapleton's First Butcher, 1991

Sutherland Shire Studies
No 1, *A brief history of Sutherland Shire*, M Hutton Neve
No 2 *Sutherland Shire Council*
No 3, *Geography and Geology Aboriginal Archaeology*
No 4, *The Development of Commerce & Industry*, M. Hutton Neve
No 5, *Parks and Recreation*
No 6, *Railways (and Tramways) in the Sutherland Shire*, Peter Neve
No 7, *History of Road Transport in the Sutherland Shire*, A & F Midgley

RAHS Newsletter No. 75, November 1968

Sydney Morning Herald 13-16 & 19.1.1965; 16.1.1982; 13.1.1987; 15.1.1987; 16.1.1987; 14-15.3.1987; 24.1.1994; 29.4.1995; 29.12.1995; 28.1.1997; 5.3.1997; 8.3.1997; 16.4.1997; 19.4.1997; 14.5.1997; 19.5.1997

Sydney Water Board Journal Vol 6, No 4

Tench, Captain Watkin, *Reprint of Journal Sydney's First Four Years*, Angus & Robertson, 1961

Thomas, Bryan, *The First Fleet, Founders of the Nation of Australia*, 1981

Thompson, J E, *Engadine NSW, An Outline History*, 1956

Turbet, Peter, *The Aborigines of the Sydney District Before 1788*, Kangaroo Press, 1989

Walkabout, February 1973

Walker, John, *Two Hundred Years in Retrospect, Kurnell-Sutherland, 1770-1970*, Sutherland Shire Historical Society, 1969.

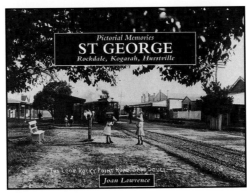